The Crusades

THE
CRUSADES

BY ANTHONY WEST

Illustrated by CARL ROSE

RANDOM HOUSE · NEW YORK

Third Printing

Copyright 1954 by Anthony West
All rights reserved under International and
Pan American Copyright Conventions
Published in New York by Random House, Inc.
and simultaneously in Toronto, Canada, by
Random House of Canada, Ltd.
Library of Congress Catalog Card Number: 54-7004
Manufactured in the U.S.A.

Contents

1 Before the Crusades   3
2 Peter the Hermit Sets Out   9
3 The Siege of Xerigordon   21
4 A Crusader Wins a Crown   44
5 On to Jerusalem   58
6 The Second Crusade   73
7 Saladin Recaptures the Holy City   87
8 Two Kings Turn Crusader   93
9 Richard Becomes the Lionhearted   106
10 The Last Wild Fight for Jaffa   130
11 The Fourth Great Pilgrimage   144
12 The Crusades of Saint Louis   160
13 After the Crusades   173
Index   181

The Crusades

1

Before the Crusades

WHEN THE FIRST CRUSADE WAS LAUNCHED IN 1095, almost a thousand years ago, the world was a very different place from the one we know. Christianity was not a great world faith then, but was hemmed in by enemies in western and southern Europe.

In its first centuries the Christian religion spread rapidly through the lands of the old Roman Empire round the Mediterranean and in western Europe. Then its spread slowed down. The peoples who lived on the northern frontiers of the old Empire were slow to accept the new faith, and before their conversion was complete

3

*The Christian religion spread rapidly
through Europe.*

they were conquered and overrun by barbarians
from the east and far north. The barbarians
swept on southwards into the ancient Roman
lands, destroying their peace and prosperity and
throwing everything into disorder and anarchy.
In these troubled times the Church lost ground
and the Christian lands shrank southwards.

4

When the Church was at its weakest, it was challenged by a new rival from the Southeast. Mohammed was born in 570 A.D. and when he was in his early thirties he began to preach the new religion of Islam. It spread like wildfire through the Arab peoples. The word *Islam* means surrender; and the word *Moslems*, which describes its believers, means "self-surrender." The Arabs gave themselves up to the new faith body and soul, and believed implicitly in their prophet's promise that all who died in battle for the new religion would go straight to a heaven where all their wishes would be granted them. The religion was a fine one for a warrior people, and with it to unite them they were irresistible for a time. Their conquering armies swept through all the old Roman provinces east and south of the Mediterranean. In two hundred years they conquered Syria, Egypt, all North

5

Africa, and Spain. Altogether they seized a third of the Christian world.

As the centuries went by, the barbarians who had swept into the Christian lands from the east and north became civilized and Christian. The Church recovered its moral force, and began to recover lost ground and win new territory. About a century before the First Crusade, Denmark, Norway, and Sweden were converted, and sixty or seventy years before it, Poland and Hungary became Christian. The Christians moved over from the defensive to the offensive. In the North, Christian kings fought against the pagans on the shores of the Baltic, and in the South, the French and Spaniards began to drive the Moslems out of Spain.

Just as the tide seemed to be turning, Christendom suffered a terrible setback. The centuries which had civilized the barbarians in Europe had also civilized the Moslem Arabs. They were no longer desert people, but softer, cultured city people. But their missionaries had converted a warrior people called the Turks from central Asia, and now they swept through the Arab lands and made themselves a ruling race. The old power of Islam as a fighter's creed was renewed in the Turks, and before long they were a serious threat to the Christians of the East.

Ever since the first appearance of the Arab conquerors, the ancient city of Byzantium or Constantinople had been the bastion that prevented the Moslems from breaking out of Asia through the Balkans, into Europe. Its Christian kings had carried on the Roman tradition of good government, and Byzantium was the richest and most prosperous kingdom in Europe. Most of its wealth and most of its fine soldiers came from the provinces it held in Asia Minor, between the Mediterranean and the Black Sea.

Now the Turks overran these provinces. The Byzantines beat them back in two campaigns, and in the third suffered a complete disaster at the Battle of Manzikert. All their trained troops were lost and for a time the kingdom was defenseless. The Turks moved in and helped themselves to such great Christian cities as Antioch and Nicea. A Turkish Sultan set himself up at Nicea and took the title Sultan of Rome.

The news spread through Christian Europe. All its great churchmen and statesmen could see that if there was little danger to Christendom in the rapidly weakening Moslem kingdoms in Spain, there was a new and dangerous threat in the East from the Turks. The Crusades were their answer to the threat.

8

2

Peter the Hermit Sets Out

WHO PETER THE HERMIT WAS OR WHERE HE CAME from nobody quite knows. Some people say he was a merchant, other people say he was a small landowner. But whatever he was, he sold everything he had when he was about thirty years old and he set out on a pilgrimage to the Holy Sepulchre at Jerusalem. Every year thousands of people all over Christian Europe set out for the Holy Land to worship at the Church of the Sepulchre, and to see the places where Christ walked on earth. They had done so for centuries, even after the Moslem Arabs had captured Jerusalem about six hundred years after the death of Christ. The

Moslems respected Christ as a true prophet of God, and they allowed Christians to have churches and monasteries in Jerusalem. They collected a small tax from each Christian pilgrim, but otherwise they did nothing to interfere with them. So Peter did not expect to have any trouble on the road when he set out.

But as he came nearer to the Holy Land, he began to hear disturbing stories. At the inns on the pilgrim roads he met men and women returning home in disappointment. They had been turned back on the way. When he reached the Christian towns on the edge of the Moslem lands, he found them full of Christian refugees who had been driven out of Jerusalem. They told him that the Arabs had been conquered and that everything was changed in the Holy Land. Arab missionaries had spread the religion of

10

Mohammed north and east into Asia, and the converts they had made there, the Kurds and Turks, had come south and made themselves masters of the Arabs. Like many converts they were more fanatical about their new religion than the people who had converted them. They were shocked to find Christians living peacefully among Moslems, and churches standing alongside mosques. They had driven the monks and priests out of Jerusalem and burned or destroyed its churches. Few Christian pilgrims were allowed to visit the Holy City.

Peter couldn't believe what he heard. He had to see for himself. So he went on. Somewhere on the road to Jerusalem he was caught. The Turks stripped him and beat him and sent him back. He begged his way to Constantinople, and somehow made his way to Rome. He had made up

11

his mind to beg the Pope to call on all Christians to fight a Holy War to free the Holy Sepulchre from the Moslems.

The Pope listened to Peter's story thoughtfully. Not long before, ambassadors had come to him from the Christian ruler of the Byzantine Empire. They had told him that the Turks—or Saracens—were too strong for the Byzantines to fight all by themselves. Their emperor, Alexius, wanted the rest of Christendom to help him to keep the Moslems out of Christian lands.

Before his election the Pope had been prior of the great monastery of Cluny in France. For over a hundred years the monks of Cluny had taken a leading part in persuading French knights not to fight each other. They urged them to go south to help the Christians in Spain to recover their lands from the Moslems. So the

12

idea of a Holy War was not a new one. The Emperor's appeal and Peter's story together convinced the Pope that it was time to attack the Moslems in the east. So he gave Peter a papal commission to preach the Holy War. The Pope himself set out for France to announce it at a great congress of cardinals, archbishops, bishops and priests that was due to take place at Clermont.

On his way to Clermont the Pope went through Provence and met Raymond of Toulouse who had often led war bands into Spain to fight the Moslems. Raymond promised to go to the Holy Land and became the first of the nobles to join the Crusade.

By the time the Pope reached Clermont, rumors of his business had spread all through France, and great masses of people had gathered. The Pope had meant to proclaim the war in a church, but the crowd was much too large to get inside any building in Clermont. So he spoke from a platform set up in the open fields east of the town. When they heard what he had to say, a wild excitement swept through the thousands of people. They were willing to go. "God wills it!" they cried, *"Dieu le veult!"* And thousands of them took an oath to serve in God's army then and there.

It was a good time to gather men for such an adventure. Three bad harvests in a row had brought ruin to many farmers and peasants. They had heard of many men who had gone to the wars against the Moslems in Spain and won themselves good farms beyond the Pyrenees. The Pope had told them that the lands taken from the Saracens would be divided among

14

those who wished to stay in the Holy Land, and it seemed like a chance to leave poverty and hardship behind. Jerusalem was the golden city at the heart of the promised land—the land of the covenant that the Bible described as flowing with milk and honey. They were eager to go.

When the Pope went back to Rome, he left two men behind him to raise the army—Peter the Hermit and Adhemar de Monteil, Bishop of Le Puy.

Adhemar was a great prince of the Church who dressed like a courtier in fur-lined cloaks and gowns made of rich materials. He had often fought in wars between nobles, and he was a famous fighter. His arms and armor were the finest that could be had; he had a wonderful helmet studded with jewels; and he even wore gold spurs. Some warrior priests carried clubs

15

or maces into battle so that they would be technically free of the sin of shedding blood, but Adhemar made no bones about carrying a great two-handed sword.

He was a soldier and made soldier-like plans. He would not accept the services of men who were too old or too young or too sick to be of real use. And he refused to enroll men who would not support their families while they were on the Crusade. He arranged for the Church to manage the money affairs of the men who were accepted. He made his appeal for recruits to a particular kind of man—the knights who had been trained in the use of arms.

Adhemar de Monteil went all over western Europe, from castle to castle, recruiting these tough fighting men. Some of them were Normans from the Channel Coast, like Baldwin of

16

Boulogne and Robert of Normandy, descendants of the sea rovers from Norway and Sweden. Others like Raymond of Toulouse were descendants of the Goths, who had settled in southern

Adhemar de Monteil made his appeal to knights who had been trained in the use of arms.

France in the troubled times when the Roman Empire was falling apart. Others again like the golden-haired Godfrey de Bouillon came from Lorraine and Burgundy where a Germanic people, the Franks, had settled. They swore an oath to Adhemar or his commissioners to stay with the Christian army until Jerusalem was free. Every man who took the oath had a cross of red material stitched to the shoulder of his cloak or surcoat. Taking the oath became known as "taking the cross," and the men who had pledged themselves were called Crusaders.

Peter the Hermit was very different from these knights. He went bare armed and barefoot in all kinds of weather, wearing nothing but a woolen smock and a light cloak that served him as a blanket at night. His beard came down to his waist, and his uncut hair tumbled over his ears and neck. He was small and miserably thin. He never ate bread or meat and took only watered wine and a few scraps of fish. He was no man to impress great lords and nobles, and he made no attempt to speak to them in their halls and castles.

Peter preached in the little villages and market towns to the peasants and poor folk. They were fascinated by his eyes, blazing like coals in his lean yellow face. They listened to him and loved him. They called him "Kiokio"—little Peter—and when he told them to leave their homes and set out for Jerusalem, they did so. They sold their farms and their houses, bought themselves bows and swords that they hardly knew how to use, put their belongings into carts, and followed him

19

with their wives and children. They had no idea how far they were going, and at every new place they asked if they had arrived in Jerusalem.

Peter led them on through northern France into Germany, preaching and gathering more people into his host. When he reached Cologne, he had assembled nearly thirty thousand men with several thousand women and children. Some poor knights—Walter Sans Avoir, Geoffrey Burel and Walter of Breteuil—had joined him and served as his commanders, but most of his followers were peasants who knew nothing of war. A few of them were wastrels, thieves, and robbers who attached themselves to him in the hope of easy pickings, and it was these few evil men who ruined Peter's hopes in the end.

3

The Siege of Xerigordon

PETER THE HERMIT HAD MADE COLOGNE THE starting point for his Crusade because it was the beginning of the old overland trail that had been followed by pilgrims going to the Holy Land for centuries. It ran up the Rhine Valley to Mainz, then turned off to follow the river Main as far as Nürnberg. There it passed through the gap between the Harz Mountains and the Erzgebirge into the Danube Valley at Regensburg. From Regensburg down the Danube to Belgrade it was easy going, but just beyond Belgrade the route turned south into the Balkan Mountains, following the Morava River up to Nish. Between

Nish and the Byzantine town of Philippopolis there was rugged mountain country, but after that it was easy going again down the Miritsa Valley through Thrace, to Constantinople. The marching distance from end to end of the road was almost 1500 miles.

Walter Sans Avoir was a level-headed man, and he knew how hard it would be to get Peter's mob of peasants and adventurers moving along this winding and difficult road. He was eager to get going so he pressed Peter to make the earliest possible start. But Peter was blind to the difficulties and to the dangers of letting his motley host stay too long in one place. He wanted to raise more German recruits.

Walter refused to wait and set out in mid-April with about six thousand of the French. He hustled his army along and arrived at Constan-

tinople in the last days of July. This was a
promising start.

Peter the Hermit and twelve or fifteen thousand men, women, and children from France
and Germany moved off toward the end of April.
The women and children rode in farm carts and
wagons drawn by horses or oxen; the men
walked or rode horseback. People who saw them
go by, straggling in disorder, said that it looked
as if all the world were moving east. Rumors
spread ahead of them saying that there were
hundreds of thousands of them, and that they
were stripping the places they passed through
like a plague of locusts.

The Hungarians waited for them with suspicion. Walter Sans Avoir's army had behaved
badly only once. That was in Hungary, at the
town of Semlin across the Danube from Bel-

It looked as if all the world were moving east.

grade. When Walter's people got there, they were short of food. The harvest had not been gathered, and there was no food in the markets. In desperation some of the Crusaders had robbed farms around the town. Others had tried to loot the shops. The raid on the shops touched off a street fight in which several men were killed. The Hungarians were afraid that worse things might happen when Peter the Hermit's much larger group arrived.

Peter's followers began pouring into Semlin

late in June. Food was as scarce as ever, and the atmosphere grew tense. The Hungarian governor of the town, who happened to be a Saracen mercenary soldier, forbade the Crusaders to come inside the walls. He issued special regulations designed to prevent clashes between them and the citizens. But these only annoyed everybody. After a couple of days a row broke out in the market between a Crusader and a townsman who couldn't agree over the price of a pair of shoes. Within a few minutes stalls were being overturned, and a riot had begun. The governor sent soldiers to break it up. When Peter's lieutenant, Geoffrey Burel, heard that some of his men were in trouble, he issued a general call to arms and went to the rescue. When the fight was over, the Crusaders had captured the governor's castle; and all the four thousand Hungarian soldiers who had been garrisoning it were dead. It was a horrible and inexcusable massacre.

When Burel realized what had happened, he decided that he must get the Crusaders across the Danube and over into Byzantine territory as quickly as possible. If they stayed in Hungary, the Hungarian king would very soon send troops to punish them for their crime. It would have taken the few boats available several days to ferry the army over the river. So Burel set his men to work tearing the houses of Semlin apart and making rafts of their woodwork.

From across the river, the Byzantine governor of Belgrade and the citizens of the town watched what was going on in Semlin with horror. The governor had not nearly enough men with him to keep the Crusaders in order when they landed. So, leaving the few men he had to guard the ferry landing, he hurried southward to get help. The terrified citizens of Belgrade fled and hid in the mountains. When the Crusaders had butchered the Byzantine soldiers at the river crossing, they pillaged and burned the empty town.

After a seven-day march through the forests of the mountainous Morava Valley, Peter's followers came to Nish where a Byzantine general

27

with a strong army was waiting for them. The general was determined to have no nonsense. As soon as the Crusaders arrived, he arrested Geoffrey Burel and Walter of Breteuil to hold as hostages for the good behavior of the rest. He saw to it that they moved off when they had bought what supplies they needed. Up to the very last minute it seemed as if his precautions had worked and prevented serious trouble. But as the last of the Crusaders filed out of Nish, some Germans who had been in a street brawl the night before set fire to a group of wooden buildings in the suburbs. Byzantine troops immediately bore down on the tail end of the column and started to arrest everyone near the fire. Some of the Crusaders turned back to rescue their comrades, and a fight began.

Peter the Hermit, riding in the column about

a mile ahead up the road, heard a wild rumor that the Byzantines had begun a massacre of his people. He galloped back, as fast as his donkey would go, to try to find the Byzantine general and stop the fighting. But he was too late; by the time he arrived the rear guard of the crusading army was trying to take the town by storm.

The Byzantines were furious, and they hit back hard. Their general ordered his well-trained troops to attack. Peter's rabble was whipped in very short order and fled in all directions. Peter escaped by scrambling up a steep hillside with five hundred of his followers. He spent a wretched night in the woods thinking they were the only survivors. But in the next few days seven or eight thousand of his people reassembled, hungry and dejected. The fight at Nish was a disaster for Peter. About a quarter of his people were dead or had disappeared. Most of his wagons were lost, and with them the cart which carried Peter's war chest. All the money which had been raised in France and Germany to buy food and supplies for the Crusaders was lost.

The Crusaders left Nish penniless and humiliated. Byzantine cavalry rode herd on them, rounding up the stragglers and keeping them moving. They were not allowed to halt anywhere on the line of march for more than three days. To make up for the hustling, the Byzantines fed them and replaced the horses and mules which had been lost at Nish. But as the Crusaders passed rapidly down the Miritsa Valley and across Thrace, they must have felt like prisoners of war marching into captivity.

When they reached Constantinople in August,

Alexius Commenus, the Byzantine Emperor, gave them a courteous welcome. But he was horrified by the sight of Peter's ragged, unruly and badly armed mob. He knew that the Saracens would be able to cut it up without much trouble. So he told Peter he would be wise to wait in Constantinople until the knights and trained soldiers of Adhemar de Monteil's army arrived. But before long he changed his tune.

Peter's men were up to their old tricks. Constantinople was richer and more splendid than any city they had ever dreamed of, and its temptations were too great for them to resist. Though the city itself was off limits to them, they got into riots and disturbances almost every day. They tried to carry off women, steal goods, or loot church treasures in the wealthy suburbs outside the walls. By the end of a week Alexius

31

was eager to see the last of them. He put them aboard ships of the Byzantine navy and had them ferried across the Bosporus into Asia.

As soon as they were in Asia, Peter's Crusaders felt that they were in enemy territory and behaved accordingly. They pillaged every place they came to and drove off the cattle. The people they were robbing were for the most part Byzantine Christians who had already suffered badly enough at Saracen hands. It was no comfort to them to find themselves treated worse than ever by their fellow Christians. The Crusaders were turning into a robber band, and Peter was rapidly losing control of them.

As the army marched along the shore of the Sea of Marmora, quarreling broke out between the French and the Germans and Italians who had joined the Crusade at Constantinople. Their disputes soon came to a head. The German-Italian party picked an Italian lord called Rainald as their leader and refused to take further orders from Peter. Peter was still nominal leader of the French. But his followers turned more and more to Geoffrey Burel, who had acted so stupidly at Semlin. The two groups set up separate camps at Civetot, a small town in a stretch of fertile farm country where the river Dracon runs into the sea.

Geoffrey Burel was first to make a move, leading several thousand Frenchmen out of camp in the middle of September. They marched up the Dracon River valley to Nicea where the Saracen who called himself Sultan of Rome kept his court. The Sultan had few soldiers at Nicea; and when they sallied out to attack the Cru-saders, they were soon driven back inside the

33

N

IRELAND

ENGLAND

BRANDEN-BERG

COLOGNE-FIRST CRUSADE LED BY PETER, APR. 1096

MAINZ
NÜRNBERG
REGENSBURG

DOMINIONS OF THE ANGEVINS (ENGLAND)

FRANCE & VASSAL STATES

KINGDOM OF GERMA

AUSTRI

LEON

PORTUGAL

NAVARRE

TOULOUSE (FRANCE)

CASTILE

ARAGON

ITALY

VENICE

CORSICA

ROME

APULI (TO S

DOMINIONS OF THE ALMOHADES (MOORS)

SARDINIA

WHERE RICHARD I QUARRELED WITH PHILIP AUGUSTUS—1191

SICILY

DOMINIONS OF THE ALMOHADES

TUNIS WHERE LOUIS IX DIED 1270

Europe around the end of the 1100s showing the route of the First Crusade under Peter the Hermit and other information

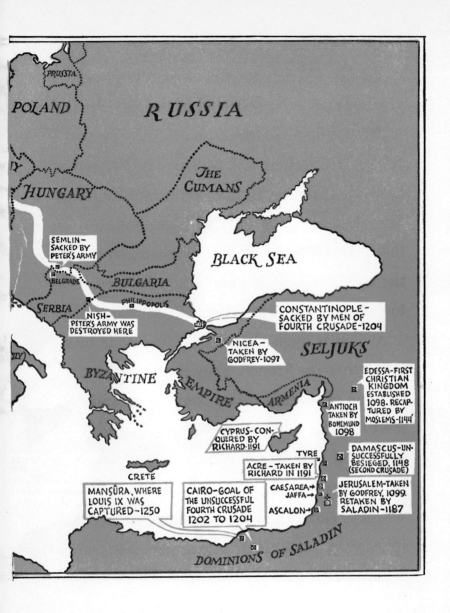

PRUSSIA

POLAND

RUSSIA

HUNGARY

THE CUMANS

SEMLIN-
SACKED BY
PETER'S ARMY

BELGRADE

BULGARIA

BLACK SEA

SERBIA

PHILIPPOPOLIS

NISH-
PETER'S ARMY WAS
DESTROYED HERE

CONSTANTINOPLE-
SACKED BY MEN OF
FOURTH CRUSADE-1204

NICEA-
TAKEN BY
GODFREY-1097

SELJUKS

BYZANTINE

EMPIRE

ARMENIA

EDESSA-FIRST
CHRISTIAN
KINGDOM
ESTABLISHED
1098. RECAP-
TURED BY
MOSLEMS-1144

ANTIOCH
TAKEN BY
BOHEMUND
1098

CYPRUS-CON-
QUERED BY
RICHARD-1191

TYRE

DAMASCUS-UN-
SUCCESSFULLY
BESIEGED, 1148
(SECOND CRUSADE)

CRETE

ACRE - TAKEN BY
RICHARD IN 1191

CAESAREA→
JAFFA→

JERUSALEM-TAKEN
BY GODFREY, 1099.
RETAKEN BY
SALADIN-1187

MANSÛRA, WHERE
LOUIS IX WAS
CAPTURED-1250

CAIRO-GOAL OF
THE UNSUCCESSFUL
FOURTH CRUSADE
1202 TO 1204

ASCALON→

DOMINIONS OF SALADIN

walls. The French went back to Civetot with a great deal of spoil collected in the suburbs and with huge flocks of sheep and cattle. This made Rainald's Germans and Italians jealous, and at the end of the month they too went off raiding. They looked at the walls of Nicea and, finding the place much too strong for them, by-passed the town. They marched on into Saracen territory looking for easy plunder.

At first it seemed as if they had done much better than the French. They surprised the small garrison of a castle called Xerigordon and took it without much trouble. The place looked like a fine prize. It had been used as an armory and a supply base by the Sultan, and it was full of weapons and stores. Rainald sent back a boastful message to Civetot saying that Xerigordon was so well set up that he was going to use it as his base for further raids into the Sultan's lands. Nobody gave much thought to the fact that all its water had to be brought in, either from a well outside the main gate or from springs at the foot of the rocky hill on which it was built.

The Turks who came to recapture Xerigordon on the twenty-ninth of September made no attempt to take the place by storm. They simply drove Rainald's people inside the walls and sat down to guard the well and the path to the springs.

Days went quietly by with no fighting. Every drop of water in the castle was gone. The Crusaders in the castle went down into the dungeons and sucked the moist earth from the floors and the dank walls in the hope of getting a few drops of moisture. They even killed their horses and mules and drank the blood in their desperation.

37

At the end of eight days there was no fight left in them, and they gave up.

The Turks allowed the Crusaders who would be converted to the Moslem faith to live; those who refused to renounce Christianity were killed. Rainald and most of his men became Moslems. The Turks sent them to Aleppo and Antioch to be sold in the slave markets. None of them were ever heard of again.

The Sultan made good use of Rainald's folly. He sent spies down into the Crusaders' camp at Civetot to tell the story that Rainald had captured Nicea and was taking vast quantities of plunder in the town. At the same time he set ambushes in the narrow gorges of the Dracon River through which the road from Civetot passed.

By this time Peter the Hermit had lost all pretense to being the leader of the French. He had gone back to Constantinople to try to get Alexius to send him some trained troops to keep his people in order. Walter Sans Avoir was still at Civetot and loyal to Peter, but the soldiers preferred Geoffrey Burel as a leader. Walter didn't believe the news that Rainald was in Nicea, and begged the Crusaders to wait until Peter returned before setting out for the city. Geoffrey Burel wanted to leave at once so that the French should get a share of the loot.

The real story of what had happened to Rainald at Xerigordon came to Civetot as the Crusaders were getting ready to march, but this only made Geoffrey more determined than ever to set out for Nicea. He said that Xerigordon had to be avenged, and that it would be cowardly and foolish not to try to wipe out the disgrace

39

with a victory. Walter Sans Avoir's objections were brushed aside.

Every man who could bear arms left the camp with Geoffrey Burel. Only old men, women, children, and the sick were left in Civetot. The Crusaders marched as if they were going to a picnic—in loose order, without scouts or flank guards. They went straight into a trap, almost within sight of their starting point. The Turks were in force only three miles away at the village of Dracon. They were hidden where the river and the road to Nicea passed through a narrow cleft between steep, thickly wooded hillsides.

The long column of the Crusaders wound into the ravine. The knights and horsemen rode at ease up in front, with their shields slung over their shoulders, their helmets and their heavy arms and armor still strapped to the saddles of

40

their baggage horses. The foot soldiers came along behind them laughing and talking.

The Turks held their fire until the last moment. Then a shower of arrows killed a quarter of the Christian knights and killed or maimed half the horses. Walter Sans Avoir and the best of the knights died well, fighting it out where they were surprised. Geoffrey Burel wheeled his horse round and led the flight of the cowards. The escaping knights, mixed up in a stampede of wounded and riderless horses, galloped through the column of foot soldiers behind them, throwing it into even wilder confusion just as the Saracens attacked. Within seconds the whole army was on the run. The Saracens followed, cutting them down in their tracks like beasts.

Three thousand men, led by a few wounded knights, managed to reach the little castle at

41

Geoffrey Burel wheeled his horse and led the flight of cowards.

Civetot, and held out there. All the rest, some six or seven thousand men, were butchered. The old men and the sick in the camp were killed, too, and the women and children sold into slavery.

Alexius sent a fleet to rescue the survivors in

the castle at Civetot and fetched them back to Constantinople. They were disarmed and given quarters where they could wait for the other Crusaders to arrive. They seem to have had the tar knocked out of them. At least, they caused the Byzantines no more trouble with their riots and brawlings.

They served the Crusaders as infantry later on, but the knights did not think much of them, to judge by the name they gave their leader— *Le Roi Truand,* King of the Bums. They swarmed along in the wake of the army, in rags and cracked shoes, with little sacks of gear hung around their necks, burned brown with the sun. They kept themselves alive by looting, thieving among the tents, and robbing the dead on the battlefields. When disease and famine hit the armies, they were the first to suffer. Few, if any, of them found their way back to their homes.

43

4

A Crusader Wins a Crown

THE KNIGHTS, BARONS AND NOBLES WHO HAD taken the cross from Adhemar de Monteil began to gather at Constantinople soon after the end of Peter's Crusade. Emperor Alexius hoped for better things from them, but he was soon disappointed. The first noble to arrive was a younger son of the King of France. He sent a pompous message ahead of him claiming a royal welcome. But while he was crossing the Adriatic Sea, his ships ran into a storm and he was shipwrecked. So he arrived at the Emperor's court without anything more than the clothes he stood up in. The knights he had brought with him were an unsavory lot. Among them were several Germans who had been bandits before they became Crusaders. This lordling and his band didn't look altogether trustworthy, so Alexius politely but firmly locked them up where they couldn't get into any trouble.

The next party of Crusaders to reach Constantinople was led by Godfrey de Bouillon. He was a tall, enormously strong man, whose golden hair and beard made a great impression on the dark Byzantines. He was a rich man, and he had brought with him about eight thousand men. Alexius liked the look of him much better. But Godfrey didn't like the look of Alexius, and he didn't like finding the French King's son in prison. He didn't like having to pay for his army's food either. He felt that, as he had come out to fight the Saracens for Alexius, the Emperor

45

*Godfrey de Bouillon made a great impression
on the Byzantines.*

ought to feed his men. But the Emperor cut off his supplies on the principle of no money, no food. As a result Godfrey's men began pillaging the suburbs, and during Easter Week they actually attacked the town. The Byzantine army fought them and drove them back to their camp. Soon afterward Alexius shipped them across the Straits to get rid of them.

And so it went on. Every new batch of Crusaders brought more trouble down on the Byzantines. The men from the south of France led by Raymond of Toulouse sacked and burned the Byzantine town of Roussa. Alexius scarcely knew if the Crusaders had come as allies or invaders. He was very glad to see the last of them when they moved off into Asia Minor.

At last the forces of the various leaders were all assembled at Chalcedon across the Straits from Constantinople. By then the Crusaders were about 40,000 strong. This included knights, archers, men-at-arms, and the cooks, bakers, grooms, blacksmiths, and armorers who saw to the needs of the fighters.

They marched past unlucky Civetot, where they saw the scattered bones of Peter's followers, came to Nicea, and laid siege to it. The Sultan of Nicea was away when they arrived, but he was in no hurry to come back, even though his wife, his children and his treasury were inside the town. He thought he had to deal with another mob like Peter's, and he didn't think he'd have any trouble driving them off. He let a month go by before he returned. When he arrived, he showed how little he thought of the Christians by attacking them at once, without resting his

48

men or their horses. He just rode up to the Christian camp and straight at it.

The Crusaders were just as straightforward. When they saw the mass of Saracen cavalry coming for them, they lined up, set their long lances in rest, and charged. They went through the Sultan's horsemen like a knife going through butter. The Saracens had never met anything like the heavily armored knights in battle before. The whole idea of the heavy lance was new to them.

The Saracens were really mounted infantry, and they were used to fighting with swords and bows on horseback. They were dressed lightly, and they were lightly armed. They had good steel helmets on their heads, light shirts of chain mail, gauntlets, and shin guards. Their shields

49

were small, round leather targets with a metal stud in the center about the size of a saucer. Their swords were made of finer steel than the great broadswords of the Crusaders, but they were half the length or less and barely heavy enough to cut through the heavy mail of the knights' hauberks. The Christians' broadswords sheered through the Saracens' flimsy mail and light shields as if they were cutting paper. And there was nothing the Saracens could do except run when the Christians rode at them with their lances.

The Sultan's men rallied several times; but as soon as they formed up, the Crusaders came thundering down on them and smashed through their ranks. The Sultan was bewildered by the Christian tactics, and stunned by his losses. He fell back into the shelter of the mountains and left Nicea to its fate.

50

The Saracens in the town were ready to surrender when they saw him go. But the Crusaders
made a bad mistake the day after the battle.
They cut off the heads of all the Saracens they
had killed in the fight and flung them over
the walls. This was meant to scare the defenders
into surrendering at once, but all it did was to
convince them that the Crusaders were barbarians. So they secretly got in touch with the
Byzantines and arranged to surrender to them.

One morning when the Crusaders woke up
they had a surprise. The Byzantine banners were
flying over the castle of Nicea and on every
tower in the city. The Emperor's troops had
slipped into the town during the night. The Crusaders were angry enough at having this rich
prize snatched from under their noses, but they
were even more angry at the way the Emperor
treated his prisoners.

The Emperor was used to fighting wars in Asia where an enemy one year might be an ally the next, helping fight an army which had been friendly a couple of years back. A ruler never knew when he might need an enemy as a friend. So it was best not to create bitterness even when things seemed going his way. So Alexius allowed the Saracens in Nicea to pay reasonable ransoms and go free. He sent the Sultan's wife and children to Constantinople as his honored guests.

The Crusaders could not understand this. They were Christians who had come to fight Moslems, and for them it was war to the knife. They were appalled by the Emperor's softness and suspected him more than ever of treachery.

Alexius tried to win their good will by sharing the greater part of the Sultan's treasure with

52

them. But his rich gifts only annoyed the Crusaders still more. They felt he was giving them what was theirs by right.

The Sultan fought them once again when they had set out on the road across the center of Asia Minor leading to Antioch. He picked a good place, where the road ran over barren, waterless country and the wells were few and far between. He knew the Crusaders would have to split their force into two or more parts to get through the desert. If they tried to get through together, the roadside wells would not be able to supply them. So he waited for them by a river at the end of the desert road hoping to deal with them piecemeal. His plan nearly succeeded.

The Crusaders had sent their archers and foot soldiers through the desert first. They stood the Sultan's army off for a whole day, chiefly because

53

The Christians' bows were longer and they shot their arrows farther.

the Christians had better bows than the Saracens. Their bows were longer from tip to tip, and they shot their arrows farther. The Christians could kill a man at any distance up to two hundred and forty yards with their long bows, while the Saracens could not kill much beyond a hundred and sixty yards. But even with this superiority the men-at-arms had had a hard time. By evening, when the knights arrived, most of them were wounded; and they were suffering cruelly from lack of water. A charge by the knights turned the scales, and the Sultan's army made off into the hills leaving hundreds of dead on the field.

The Crusaders had no more trouble from the Sultan, but they had a great deal of trouble from the climate. In July, August and September, they were tormented by heat and thirst. Then in October, as they made their way through the gorges of the Taurus Mountains, the rains came. The trampling of thousands of men and horses turned the narrow mountain tracks into mires of liquid mud. Dozens of horses slipped in the

55

slime and slid helplessly into ravines. Hundreds of mules, loaded with baggage, went the same way. Flash floods swept over the roads and through the camps doing more damage. It was a miserable journey.

While the Crusaders were slithering and sliding through the mountains, some strangers came to meet them. They fell in with Baldwin of Boulogne and asked him to come to their help. They were Armenian Christians from the little Kingdom of Edessa, not far off to the east in the Euphrates Valley. Their kingdom had been conquered not long before by the Sultan of Rome. The Armenians thought that as the Crusaders had beaten the Sultan twice and captured his capital, it would be a good time to try to win back their freedom. They asked Baldwin to help them. He turned aside with eighty knights and

56

a few hundred men-at-arms to see what could be done. He cleared the kingdom of Saracens without much trouble, and in the following March the Armenians crowned Baldwin as the King of Edessa. He was the first of the Crusaders to win himself a crown.

5

On to Jerusalem

THE CRUSADERS WERE ASTONISHED BY ANTIOCH when they got there. Its walls were miles around, and they were guarded by four hundred towers. The web of its streets spread over a space three miles long and a mile wide, and most of its buildings were made of cut stone. It made Paris and the towns the Crusaders knew, with their wooden houses and narrow twisting alleys, seem like villages in comparison.

Antioch was a rich town, too. For fifteen hundred years merchants from India and Persia had come there to meet traders from Egypt, Greece, and Rome to buy and sell their goods. There was

58

gold in the gravels washed down to Antioch by the river Orontes, and copper in the hills near by. The soil was fertile, and forests of cedars grew not far off. It had been fought for by many kings and emperors, and it had seen many gods come and go. Some of its Christian churches had been temples of Diana and Apollo, and the old Syrian fish goddess still had shrines on the seacoast, though the Moslems, changing her name and sex, called her the Sheik of the Sea.

Because it had known so many gods and goddesses in its long history, Antioch had become tolerant. Moslems and Christians lived side by side within its walls and worshiped after their own fashions without interfering with each other. To the Crusaders it seemed as if the Christians of Antioch had made a bargain with the devil.

59

They had a hard time capturing the city. They arrived late in the year, and they found that the Saracens had gathered all the crops and taken every scrap of food and fodder in the neighborhood into their stores inside the walls. The defenders of Antioch ate well while the Crusaders starved on the plain outside. By Christmas there was famine in the Christian camp, and men and horses died of hunger. But there was no going back across the mountains and deserts to Constantinople; they would starve for certain if they tried to retreat. So they hung on, making sure that no food went into Antioch, hoping that before hunger beat them it would make the Saracens surrender the city.

While the test of endurance went on and a year went by, one Saracen army after another came to try to save the city. One Saracen army came from Damascus, then another from Aleppo, and last of all a huge force from Mosul in the distant valley of the Tigris. Luckily, two days before the Saracens from Mosul arrived, the Crusaders captured Antioch. From its walls they looked out over the plain and saw the largest Saracen army of all pouring down the roads from the hills. They realized what a narrow escape they had had.

But it was a case of "out of the frying pan and into the fire." The Saracens from Mosul tried to retake the city. Hunger had defeated the Saracens in Antioch, and there was no food left in the town. When the Crusaders saw that it was their turn to stand a siege, they searched every nook and cranny for hidden stores of grain; but they found practically nothing. They stewed leaves from the trees, and chewed harness

61

The Crusaders captured Antioch.

leather. They had nearly been beaten by hunger when the besieging army began to break up. The Saracen leaders had quarreled among themselves, and the patience of their followers was worn out by waiting about while the Crusaders starved. Larger and larger groups of Saracens deserted every day and rode off to their distant homes. At last one day the Crusaders looked out and saw that the Saracen army had so dwindled away that they could go out and fight on level terms.

When the Saracens saw the knights riding out to challenge them, their leader tried to protect his men from a charge by setting fire to the dried grass in front of his battle line. But the knights charged straight through the fire. When the Saracens saw them bursting through the wall of smoke and flame, they turned and ran. The Cru-

63

saders chased them down to the banks of the river Orontes, killing them until they were tired of swinging their swords. The Saracen survivors made no attempt to come together as an army and went back to Mosul.

This victory opened the road south to Jerusalem. But it was a long time before the Crusaders took it. They stayed in Antioch wrangling over which of their leaders it was to belong to. Bohemond of Taranto and Raymond of Toulouse both wanted it and neither would give way to the other. They argued while July, August, September, October, and November went by. At last they reached a compromise. A council of nobles and bishops would decide who was to be Prince of Antioch when Jerusalem was captured. Both men agreed. But, as neither man would trust the other out of his sight, this did not get matters much further. Raymond was not going to march his followers off down the Jerusalem road while Bohemond stayed in Antioch, for he knew his rival would grab the town as soon as he was gone. And Bohemond was just as determined not to leave Raymond behind him to take possession the minute his back was turned.

While this wrangle was going on the Crusaders had to fight a worse enemy than the Saracens. But their weapons and their courage were of no use against this enemy. The priests and knights prayed for deliverance while typhoid fever cut down the Christians by the hundreds. Adhemar de Monteil, dozens of the best knights, and thousands of men-at-arms died. Out of a band of fifteen hundred Germans who came out to join the Crusade just after the capture of Antioch, only a hundred survived to march on to Jerusalem. The

65

camp followers and the remains of Peter the Hermit's band were almost wiped out.

But at last Raymond's hands were forced. His knights came to him in a body and told him that they would leave him if he didn't carry out his vows to go to liberate the Holy Sepulchre at Jerusalem. So in January Raymond marched out his men, followed by the companies of Godfrey de Bouillon and Robert of Normandy. As soon as they were gone, Bohemond closed the gates and hoisted his banners everywhere in the city. A short while later he proclaimed himself Prince of Antioch. And so the second Christian kingdom was set up by the Crusaders. Raymond rode on toward Jerusalem as the leader of the Crusade, hoping for the third crown.

The Crusaders had started on a long and weary march down the coast of Palestine. They

66

*Ierusalem was the strongest fortress of
the ancient world.*

went past the snow-capped mountains of Lebanon, past the ancient cities of Tyre and
Sidon, past Acre and Jaffa. There they turned
inland. Six months after they left Antioch, they
reached the crest of the pass through the mountains which stand between Jerusalem and the
sea and camped there for the night. During the
hours of darkness they were heartened by an
eclipse of the moon, which they took as a sign
that the Christian cross would soon overcome the
crescent that the Moslems had made their sym-
bol. The next morning they climbed a hill called
Montjoie in the chilly gray light before dawn. As
the sun rose, they looked down on Jerusalem.

The sight filled them with a mixture of joy and
horror. They had expected to find the Promised
Land, flowing with milk and honey, on the far
side of the bare hills they had just climbed. But a

68

bare, dusty valley, baked brown by the summer heat, lay in front of them. And Jerusalem was the strongest fortress of the ancient world.

It stood on a hill, and its walls crowned the steep sides of three rocky valleys. For two thousand years ruler after ruler of Jerusalem had done his best to make the fortress impregnable. And they had done their work well. But as the Christians approached the city, a frenzy of determination took hold of them. Nothing was going to stop them. When they camped under the walls, they found that the Saracens had filled in the wells for miles in every direction. The Crusaders stayed where they were and brought water in wineskins on pack mules from as far off as the Jordan Valley. It arrived brackish and foul at the end of the long journey in the baking heat, but it was good enough. The Crusaders endured for thirty days, and at the end of the month fought their way into the city.

As darkness fell on their day of triumph, their fighting frenzy turned into a madness. All through the night they searched the town, killing every man, woman, and child they could find. Many of the Jews of the Holy City had taken refuge in the chief synagogue, but there was no safety for them there. It was burned over their heads, and those who ran out to escape the flames were cut down. Every one of them died. Toward morning the Crusaders made their way to the great mosque called The Dome of the Rock where all the Saracens had been imprisoned after they had surrendered and handed over their weapons. The Crusaders killed them all. When daylight came, Jerusalem was stained with blood and more than twelve thousand people were dead in its streets and mosques. The memory of this massacre created a bitterness that lasted for century after century.

The Crusaders had won Jerusalem, and their oath to free the Holy Sepulchre from the infidel had been fulfilled. They were free to go home. But before they went, they had to choose a guardian and defender of the Holy City. Raymond of Toulouse waited for them to fulfill his ambitions and to bestow the crown of the new Christian kingdom upon him. But he was sixty-five, and a bout of typhoid that he had suffered at Antioch had left him frail and weakened. The choice of the Council of Knights fell on Godfrey de Bouillon, a younger man who had been one of the first to fight his way into Jerusalem. He had not quarreled with Bohemond at Antioch, either, and that tipped the scale in his favor. If the Saracens tried to win the Holy City back, it might be necessary for all the Christian kings in the Holy Land to stand together, and it was best to pick a king who had no old score to settle with Bohemond. And so Godfrey was the third Crusader to become a king.

6

The Second Crusade

EDESSA, THE FIRST KINGDOM SET UP BY THE Crusaders, was the first to fall. The Emir of Mosul captured its capital on Christmas Eve in 1144. He slaughtered all the Christian men he captured, and sold their wives and daughters into slavery. The news caused a panic in Antioch and Jerusalem. There were about a thousand Christian knights in the Kingdom of Jerusalem at this time, and not quite so many in Syria. If the Emir of Mosul should attack Antioch or Jerusalem with as much determination as he had shown at Edessa, the Christians would need much greater strength to hold their ground.

73

They sent despairing messages to the Pope begging him to call for a new Crusade.

Pope Eugenius was a wise man. Before he called for a second crusade, he made a study of what had happened on the first. When he had done so, he sent a message to King Louis VII of France and to the people of his kingdom, asking them to help the Christians of the Holy Land and Syria. He asked Bernard of Clairvaux in France, head of the Cistercian order of Monks, to organize the new Crusade.

Bernard was a great man, a great organizer and a saint. But he was a passionate, excitable man and, as he himself often had to admit, he sometimes let his feelings get the better of his judgment. He was determined to make the Crusade a success, and his enthusiasm upset the Pope's carefully made plans.

74

What happened was this: Bernard called a great meeting in central France at which King Louis VII and his brother Robert and a great many French barons "took the Cross" and pledged money and men for the Crusade. Bernard then went into the independent dukedoms farther north looking for more men and money. He passed through Burgundy, Lorraine and Flanders. While he was there, he heard that Conrad Hohenstaufen, the German Emperor, was not far off in the Rhineland where the Parliament of German Barons was meeting. It seemed like a heaven-sent opportunity, so Bernard hastened into Germany to preach the Crusade to this gathering. After much persuasion Conrad and his nobles "took the Cross."

Bernard was delighted with this success, and wrote to the Pope to tell him the good news. The

75

Pope was appalled. He knew that all the misfortunes that plagued the First Crusade had sprung from disputes about the leadership. It was to avoid such arguments that he had made his appeal to the French, and to the French alone, to take part in the Second Crusade. And now two kings and two kingdoms were involved. Eugenius knew that Bernard had made a terrible mistake, but it was too late to do anything about it.

The German army was first to set out a year later. It took the overland route through Hungary and across the Balkans. All went well until Conrad's men reached Byzantine territory. At the first big town they came to there was trouble. The German men-at-arms mistook a Greek conjurer for a magician and tried to burn him. The townspeople who knew his act and liked it tried

76

to protect him. A fight began in which the suburbs of the town were looted and burned. There were more fights and brawls along the line of march. Near Constantinople one of Conrad's generals revenged an attack on some of his men by burning a monastery and killing the monks who lived in it. The more Manuel, the new Emperor of Byzantium, heard about the approaching Germans, the less he liked the idea of their coming to Constantinople. He determined to head them off if he could.

He met Conrad on the road and advised him to turn aside toward the far end of the Sea of Marmora. He told the German Emperor that he would be wise to cross the Straits there, and to follow the coast road round to Antioch. He warned him not to take the inland road through Nicea that had meant so much hardship and

77

loss to the men of the First Crusade. But Conrad was determined to follow the old line of march, and suspected that Manuel was only trying to keep him away from Constantinople.

Conrad had his way. He went through Constantinople and presently set out from Nicea with his army of ten thousand men. He was back in less than a month. All his baggage was lost, and nine out of every ten of his men were dead or taken prisoner. His army had been attacked one evening after a hard day's marching through waterless desert. It was almost dark. The knights were resting; their squires were watering the horses along the banks of a river some distance from the camp; the men-at-arms were pitching tents and unloading the pack horses. Suddenly the Turkish cavalry swept down on them. The battle was all over in less than an hour. Conrad

78

was lucky to escape with his life and a thousand men.

The French took the same route as Conrad and the Germans as far as Constantinople. But they started out about a month later. When they came into Byzantine territory, they found it so stirred up by the passage of the Germans that it was like enemy country. The towns and their markets were closed to them, and they had endless difficulty raising food and supplies. The French blamed Emperor Manuel for all their difficulties, and they were already angry when they reached Constantinople. As soon as they arrived, they heard that Manuel had just signed a twelve-year truce with the Turks. It seemed to them that this gave the Turks a free hand to fight the Crusaders and the Christians in Syria.

The Bishop of Langres, one of Bernard's Cis-

79

tercians, was a fine military engineer. He immediately drew up a plan for cutting off the water supply of Constantinople and for attacking the city as an enemy town. Several of the French barons were for the Bishop's plan, but King Louis VII managed to persuade them to give it up. He even got them to take Manuel's advice, and presently they marched off toward the Holy Land by way of the coast road.

It was a terrible journey across rough country in an unusually early and severe winter. Supplies were hard to get, and the army was hungry most of the way. Turkish cavalry shadowed it, picking off stragglers, cutting up foraging parties, and raiding the camps at night. In one night raid King Louis escaped by climbing a tree and hiding while the Turkish horsemen milled around among the French tents.

When the French reached Attalia, on the south coast of Asia Minor, they were heartily sick of the running fight and decided to go the rest of the way by sea. But all the ships in the port were owned by Byzantines who charged such high prices that only the King and his barons could pay the fares. The men-at-arms had to struggle on along the coast road.

The going was much harder on this stretch. The road was worse, and the Turks had burned all the farms and villages near it. They had even driven the inhabitants inland. There was no food to be found and no shelter. More than half of Louis' soldiers died of hunger, disease, and misery between Attalia and Antioch.

When King Louis' army was at last assembled at Antioch, the Christians there wanted him to march inland to attack Aleppo. This was

81

a sensible plan because the Saracens were using that town as the base for their attacks on the Christians in Syria. But King Louis had heard that Manuel had lent Conrad ships and given him and what was left of his army passage to the Kingdom of Jerusalem. The French did not want the Germans to get to Jerusalem ahead of them. So they left Syria and hurried south to Jerusalem.

Both armies spent six months in the Holy City doing nothing except quarrel. The French jeered at the Germans for their defeat in the desert. The Germans jeered at the French barons for leaving their men to suffer and starve on the coast road. The leaders of the two armies couldn't agree on any plans for action against the Saracens. At last they decided to attack Damascus.

*The Crusaders began to quarrel
among themselves.*

This was an odd idea. The Emir of Damascus
had been neutral so far. He was no friend of
the Emirs of Mosul or of the Seljuk Turks who
had defeated Conrad's army. He had taken no

part in the attacks on the Christians in Syria, and he hadn't fought against the Kingdom of Jerusalem. All the same, the Crusaders marched off to attack him.

The siege of Damascus lasted for four days. The town was much larger than the Crusaders had expected, and they didn't have enough men to encircle it. They didn't have large enough siege engines to break down the strong walls. And as soon as the Crusaders got there, they began to quarrel among themselves about who would have it when it was taken. While they were quarreling, the Emir of Damascus discovered that he had more men inside the town than the Crusaders had outside it. So he did the attacking. He drove the Christians away without much trouble. As they retreated down the road to Jerusalem in the July heat, Saracen bowmen sniped at them continuously and killed hundreds of men and horses.

Conrad went home in a fury after this. King Louis VII spent some time dawdling around Antioch and Jerusalem, putting off the day when he had to admit his failure as a Crusader and go home with nothing to show for his long journey.

At last the French went home in disgust. They went hating the Germans as much as the Byzantines. People who have made mistakes rarely have the courage to admit it, and the Crusaders behaved like anyone else. The French blamed Conrad for losing his army south of Nicea, and all the rest of their troubles they blamed on Emperor Manuel. When they got home, they said that there ought to be a new Crusade—against Constantinople and the Emperor this

85

time. Bernard of Clairvaux, who had only the French side of the story to go on, agreed. So did the great Abbot Suger of Paris who had ruled France while the King was overseas. Pope Eugenius told them it was folly and so did Conrad. But the damage was done. The Christians were divided by mistrust and suspicion, and many of them thought the Byzantines were worse enemies than the Saracens.

As for the Saracens, they were united as they had never been before. Their great new leader Nur-ed-din began to make plans to sweep away the Kingdom of Jerusalem as Zengi had swept away the Kingdom of Edessa.

7

Saladin Recaptures the Holy City

EVERY YEAR THAT WENT BY AFTER THE FAILURE
of the Second Crusade saw things taking a worse
turn for the Christians in the Kingdom of Jerusalem. Nur-ed-din died, and for a time they
hoped that his death would divide and weaken
the Saracens. But Saladin, who took his place,
was an even greater leader. Then when Jerusalem needed him most, King Baldwin IV of Jerusalem, a brave fighter and a good leader, fell sick
and died. His son was a weak child and did not
outlive him by many months, and so the throne
of Jerusalem passed to Guy of Lusignan.

It was a bad day for Jerusalem when Guy

became king. When his brother heard that he had been crowned, he was amazed and said: "If the men who made my brother a king had known me, they would have made me a god." Guy was hot-tempered and rash. He had been banished from France for murdering a man in a quarrel. He was new to the Holy Land and knew little about fighting the Saracens. Everyone in Jerusalem told him that his only chance to hold his own against Saladin was to play a waiting game. If he stayed close to his walled towns and his castles and avoided battles in the open, there was a chance that Saladin's followers would become bored and go home. The knights who knew Saracen ways knew how hard it was to keep a Moslem army together when there was little fighting going on.

Guy would not listen. He said that nothing

would make him act like a coward. He believed that the way to beat Saladin was to go after him and bring him to battle. He marched up the Jordan Valley to Tiberias, trailing his coat through Saracen territory. Saladin fell back in front of him, letting him get farther and farther from his strongholds. At last when the Christians had been lured on far enough, Saladin swung around between them and the road home and penned them up in a dry valley. Guy had put himself in a terrible position. He had with him almost all the fighting men in his kingdom, and he had taken the True Cross from the Holy Sepulchre in Jerusalem to serve as a battle standard. Everything he had was at stake, and he hadn't a chance.

From the scrubby hillside on which his army was trapped, his men could look down into a

89

green valley where a lake sparkled and gleamed. But there was not a drop of water on the hillside. It was a hot, windless day in the beginning of July, and the sun beat down on the Christians mercilessly. During the morning the Saracens set fire to the scrub all around Guy's army, and the hot, choking smoke drifted up the hillside parching their throats. But even in this hopeless position Guy and his men fought for a whole day. When the last of them surrendered, they were so exhausted by heat and thirst that they could barely stand, and some were too weak to hand over their swords to the victors. When they gave in, Saladin wept with joy. He knew that the strength of the Kingdom of Jerusalem was destroyed and that he had won back the Holy Land. He spent the rest of the summer occupying one Christian castle

Once more the Holy City was in Saracen hands.

after another, and in October he gave thanks to his god in the Mosque of Omar in Jerusalem.

Saladin was just and merciful. He spared the life of Guy of Lusignan, and he allowed the families of the Christian knights he had killed or captured to go free. He burned no Christian buildings in Jerusalem; and three days after he entered the city, he handed its churches back to Christian priests. The Holy Sepulchre was closed for three days, but then it was opened once again to Christian pilgrims.

But the fact remained. The True Cross and the Holy City were in Saracen hands. The word went back to Europe that the work of the First Crusade had been undone.

8

Two Kings Turn Crusader

WHEN THE THIRD CRUSADE BEGAN, KING RICHARD I of England and Philip Augustus of France were firm friends. When it was over, they were bitter enemies and ready to fight a savage war with each other. They were an odd pair to make friends in the first place.

Richard was a carroty-haired giant, six feet three in height, with the build of a champion athlete. When he thought of a thing, he did it at once; and he said exactly what he thought. He loved nothing better than fighting, hunting and the open air. Philip Augustus was a weedy man of poor physique who hated taking risks.

93

Richard I and Philip Augustus were an odd pair to make friends.

He loved secret plots hatched in dark corners, and his favorite game was to play off one man's ambitions and hopes against another's. It is easier to understand how they came to hate each other than how they made friends.

But friends they were when they met at Vezelay with their great armed companies to set out for the Holy Land in July, 1190. They rode off through the vineyards of Burgundy to Lyons side by side, laughing and talking together as gaily as if they were going to a tournament. At Lyons they parted. The French King went to Genoa where a fleet of Italian ships was waiting for his soldiers. Richard went down the Rhone Valley to Marseilles, where he was to meet his ships. They were to have sailed from England, across the Bay of Biscay and around Spain. But when he got to Marseilles, he found no ships there. His English soldiers and sailors had been caught up in a little war of their own on the way. They had found the Portuguese fighting the Saracens at Lisbon, and they had gone ashore to lend them a hand. They were more than a month behind their program.

95

Richard kicked his heels in idleness for a week or two at Marseilles and then got bored with waiting. He hired some fast galleys and went off sightseeing along the Italian coast. He left word for his English ships to join him at Messina in Sicily.

The galleys met his English fleet of 106 war craft and transports at sea northwest of Messina. On the following day they all sailed into the port with a great display of banners and battle flags, and much blowing of silver trumpets. The French King was on the dockside when Richard landed and gave him a warm welcome, but there was something about it that made Richard suspicious.

When the English King got to his quarters, his suspicions increased. He had been given a small house in the suburbs outside the town

walls. His men had been given a poor camp
site on the beach. The French King was in the
Royal Palace in the town, and his men were all
well housed inside its walls. Tancred, King of
Sicily, was a long way off, in Palermo, and he
had sent no message of greeting to Richard.
This did not surprise Richard. Tancred was a
usurper who had snatched the throne of Sicily
on the death of its last king, William the Good.
William had been married to an Englishwoman
who was Richard's sister Joanna. When William
died he had left a large sum of money to Richard's father, Henry II. But when Tancred seized
the throne, he had made Joanna a prisoner; and
he had put the money to his own uses. Richard
sent a brief message to Tancred, asking for his
sister and the money. Tancred sent Joanna but
no money. Richard began to suspect that Tan-

cred and Philip Augustus might be up to something and warned his men to be on their guard.

He was quite right. On October 4th Richard went to a conference to discuss plans for the Crusade with Philip Augustus and a delegation of Tancred's nobles. While Richard was at the meeting, the Sicilians quietly surrounded the English camp, closed the town gates and occupied the walls. When their preparations were complete, they tried to rush Richard's camp. But the English soldiers were all armed and ready, and they gave Tancred's Sicilians a rough reception. Within ten hours Richard had scattered the Sicilians, broken down the town gates, and begun to loot the city. Richard had told his men they could pay the Sicilians for their treachery by taking anything they could lay their hands on. The next morning Richard

98

hoisted his flag with three leopards on it over all the towers of Messina, just as if he were celebrating the capture of an enemy city.

Tancred came crawling with the money Richard had demanded. What is more, he brought letters with him which showed that Philip Augustus had proposed the attack. In a towering rage Richard went to see the French King and demanded an explanation. Philip Augustus said the letters were forgeries and clumsy ones. Then he said that Richard was only making the most of them because he had a bad conscience. He wanted an excuse to get out of marrying the French King's sister Adalais. Richard was silent. Philip Augustus told him that he knew from his spies that Richard had already asked the Spanish princess, called Berengaria, to marry him, in spite of his engagement to Adalais, and that

99

this new fiancée was on her way to Messina. Richard sulkily admitted that it was all true. Philip Augustus adroitly turned the argument from his own treason to his sister's wrongs, and in the end an agreement was patched up between them. Richard undertook to pay a large sum of money to Adalais for breach of promise. The question of whether the letters to Tancred were forgeries or not was forgotten.

The two kings spent the winter together in Messina. The French sailed for the Holy Land in the Genoese ships in March, and the English set out in April. On Good Friday, two days after they sailed, the English were scattered by a storm which drove most of their ships before it as far as Crete. When they gathered again, twenty-five ships were missing, among them two important transports. One had all Richard's money aboard, the other carried his sister Joanna and his wife-to-be, Berengaria. Richard sent light galleys out to search for them and presently located them at Limmasol on the Island of Cyprus. Three or four other English ships had been driven ashore near by. Isaac, King of Cyprus, imprisoned all survivors of the wrecks. They had been stripped of all their possessions and weren't being properly fed. He was holding the two important transports and several other English ships, as prizes. Richard went into another of his furies when he heard of this piracy and set sail for Cyprus to make short work of King Isaac.

Richard sailed into Limmasol and occupied it after a short fight. He routed Isaac's army and captured his camp on the following day. He celebrated his victory by marrying Berengaria, and immediately after the ceremony rode off to meet Isaac. It was a colorful meeting. The King of Cyprus was dressed in purple in the style of a Roman emperor, and Richard was dressed as a bridegroom in a rose-colored tunic, scarlet cap, and a dark blue cloak covered with half moons of solid silver. He had a sword with a gold hilt at his side, and as he rode up to the meeting place, he sat on a saddle of scarlet studded with gold stars. Richard had set up a handsome embroidered tent in a grove of fig trees for the meeting. It must have looked familiar to Isaac. It had belonged to him a few days before.

The meeting went well; all was friendly and easy; and the two kings exchanged the kiss of peace. But when Isaac decided it was time to go home he found that, whether he liked it or

*Fauvel was the finest charger Richard
had ever seen.*

not, he was Richard's guest. During the night
he cut his way out of the tent in which he had
been detained, found his bay horse Fauvel in
the dark, and escaped.

Richard chased poor Isaac and Fauvel all over

Cyprus in the next fifteen days, capturing all its towns and castles in the course of the pursuit. At the end of the hunt Isaac rode into Richard's camp and gave himself up. Utterly disheartened, he only asked for two things —for his life, and for Richard's promise that he wouldn't be put in irons. Richard grinned and gave his word. Then he had silver fetters made for his distinguished prisoner.

All through the pursuit Richard had been close on Isaac's heels and had almost caught him on several occasions. But Isaac had set his spurs to Fauvel's flanks each time and easily outdistanced the best of the horses that were after him. As the chase went on, Richard had become more and more eager to get Fauvel. And now that he had him, he was even more pleased with him than he was with his new kingdom. Fauvel was the finest charger he had ever seen, and he knew just what he would do with him. But he had no very clear idea what to do with the Island of Cyprus.

After he had put Isaac in his silver fetters, Richard spent eight more days in Cyprus, and then set sail for the Holy Land. He never returned. Later on he gave the Kingdom of Cyprus to Guy of Lusignan as a present, to make up for the loss of his Kingdom of Jerusalem. But he never parted with Fauvel while he was in the Holy Land, and the pair of them were remembered for centuries in Saracen poems and songs.

9

Richard Becomes the Lionhearted

WHEN RICHARD REACHED THE HOLY LAND IN June, he joined forces with Philip Augustus outside the city of Acre, where Christians had been besieging a Saracen garrison for two years.

Acre stood on a headland jutting out into the sea. Its walls crossed the neck connecting it with the mainland in an L shape. There was a great bastion which the Crusaders called the Accursed Tower at the angle of the wall. The Christian camp was outside the walls, following the line of the wall from sea to sea at some distance. Beyond the Christian camp lay Saladin's camp. The Christians hemmed in the Saracens

*Richard watched when the French made
their assault.*

in the town, and the Saracens outside it hemmed them in. The besiegers were being besieged.

When Richard looked over the Christian lines, it seemed to him that they were much too far from the town walls. As he understood siege work, close fighting did the trick. You pushed your bowmen and your stone-throwing machines as near to the walls as you could, so that they could keep up a steady fire on the defenders. The aim was to drive the enemy from their walls, so that the engineers could either knock a gap in them with rams or tunnel under the foundations and undermine them. He could see at a glance that the Christians were too far from the walls of Acre to do the garrison any real harm.

When Richard said this to the French, they told him that they knew it very well. But if they moved their big wooden stone-throwing catapults and mangonels any closer, the Saracens threw out great copper pots that burst into flame when they hit the ground. Dozens of their machines had been hit by these fire pots and burned. Philip Augustus' engineers thought they had the answer. It stood to reason that if the fire pots were made of copper, then copper would resist whatever they contained. The French were covering all their siege machines with copper plates in preparation for a new attack.

Richard watched when the French made their assault. Their chief hope was a wheeled wooden tower higher than the walls of Acre. When it was pushed close enough to the walls, the bowmen on its upper platform would be able to fire down on the defenders of the Accursed Tower. As it creaked in toward the great bastion, with its copper plates gleaming in the sunlight, the Saracens began to fire at it. One earthenware jar after another hit it and smashed. No fire broke out. As the pots broke, the colorless liquid in them splashed and ran down its sides. The French cheered. The copper plates seemed to be doing their work. More pots sailed out over the walls and smashed against the crawling tower. And still nothing seemed to happen. The liquid soaked the bowmen's clothes and the woodwork. But it did no one any harm. The French in the wooden tower began to jeer at the Saracens on the Accursed Tower as they fired their first shots down on them. Suddenly a tree trunk, blazing from end to end, sailed over the wall in a shower of sparks. It hit the tower and lay crackling beside it for a few seconds. Then a huge white flame leapt up round

110

the tower and within a minute it was a blazing ruin. Every man in it was burned alive.

The French fell back in dismay, and the attack petered out.

Philip Augustus was sickened by this failure. A few days later he took to his bed with the shivering fever which was raging in the Christian army. His cousin the Count of Flanders and hundreds of his men had died of it. And it had killed all but two hundred of several thousand men from Norway, Sweden and Denmark. Philip Augustus was afraid that he was going to die too, and he bitterly regretted ever having left France. Until then he had been the recognized leader of the Crusade. Now that he was sick and in despair, the army turned from him to Richard for leadership.

Richard caught the fever, too. But it had a

111

different effect on him. He was filled with a restless longing to be done with the siege. He ordered the English to take the Accursed Tower at all costs. He had his bed carried into the front line and lay shivering and sweating from his fever within bowshot of the falls, urging his men on. He kept a crossbow beside him in his bed so that he could fire at any Saracen who showed himself on the wall. His men protected him from the fire pots by building a shield of hides over his bed, fireproofed by being kept soaked in vinegar. While the English bowmen kept the Saracens off the wall, their miners tunneled under the foundations of the bastion, digging out the rock and replacing it with timber supports that would presently be burned away. When their work was done, they came scuttling out of their tunnels. Thick smoke boiled out after them and curled up through cracks in the ground as the fires took hold. The whole army stood watching for the tower to fall. But when the timbers were burned away, the huge mass of masonry swayed, lurched, and came to rest in one piece. It was leaning toward the Crusaders' lines, but it was still standing.

Richard watched, in one of the black furies for which he was famous, and cursed the engineers for botching the job. Then he collected himself. He shouted to his men, offering two gold pieces to every man who would bring him a stone torn out of the wall. The soldiers and miners looked up at the Saracen archers lining the battlements, and nobody moved. Four gold pieces, cried Richard. The English surged forward with picks and crowbars.

They toiled on all through the night. The

Saracens killed hundreds of Christians as they clawed at the stonework in bright moonlight, but the next day the Accursed Tower came crashing down, opening a huge breach in the wall.

The Christians rushed in. They were led by Aubrey Clement, a knight who had sworn to get into Acre that day or die. The Crusaders saw him stand alone for a moment in the breach waving them on, and then a rush of fifty or sixty Saracens was on him. A few seconds later the Christian knights stood beside his body looking down into Acre. But as they stood there, a shower of earthenware pots fell round them, soaking their surcoats and their leather hauberks with the same colorless fluid that had been poured over the French tower. The pots were followed by a flight of arrows and cross-

114

bow bolts with smouldering tinder tied to their shafts. To the Crusaders it seemed as if the rubble of the tower burst into flame all round them. Throwing aside their weapons and beating out their blazing clothes, they turned and ran. Acre still held, even though the Accursed Tower had fallen.

But the Saracens in Acre were beaten. After they had flung back Richard's attack, they took stock. Of the thirty thousand men who had been sent to hold the town by the Saracens, six thousand were left; and most of those were wounded or sick. They had used up all their fire pots and almost all their arrows. And food was running low. After two years they no longer hoped that Saladin would break through the Christian ring and relieve them. So they surrendered.

When Saladin heard that his men in Acre

115

were prisoners, he offered to ransom them. The Christians set a high price on their captives. First they wanted the True Cross, that Saladin had captured from Guy of Lusignan. Then they wanted 1,600 Christians who were in Saladin's prisons. And after that 200,000 gold pieces. The Christians were to keep their Saracens until the last man and the last penny of the ransom had been handed over.

While the Crusaders waited for Saladin to raise the ransom, they rested and quarreled. Philip Augustus, wasted by sickness and shaken by the terrible gaps that plague and war had made in the French ranks, wanted to go home. Richard wanted to go on to Jerusalem. At last the English King agreed to let the French King go if he would leave the Duke of Burgundy and ten thousand men behind to fight under him. Then there was another quarrel about who should be recognized as the King of Jerusalem. Richard wanted the crown to go back to Guy of Lusignan. The French King favored Conrad of Montferrat. The French King had his way. He forced Richard to agree by saying that unless Conrad was made King he would take the Duke of Burgundy and his army home to France with him. Richard felt he had been blackmailed; and when Philip Augustus sailed for France, he fell once again into one of his furies.

He found an ugly vent for his rage. Saladin had been given forty days to raise the ransom for the prisoners, and then more time, and then again more time. Richard suddenly decided that the Saracens were playing with him, and that he would teach them a lesson.

One day Saladin's men saw an unusual bustle

117

in the Crusaders' camp. All the Christian troops marched out and formed a battle line facing the hills where the Saracens were encamped. The Saracens stood to arms, expecting to be attacked. But the Christian line remained motionless facing them. Then the Saracens saw that a procession of Moslem prisoners, with their hands roped behind them, was being driven out of Acre. The column wound its way to the top of a small hill behind the Christian battle line. The Saracens could not understand what was happening until the column halted and the guards began cutting the throats of the helpless prisoners. The Saracens made desperate efforts to rescue their comrades, but they could not break through the Christian ranks. When the dreadful work was done, Richard ordered his army back to camp. The Saracens found 2,600 bodies on the blood-soaked hillside.

Richard soon left plague-ridden Acre and marched down the coast to Jaffa, the port which served Jerusalem. It was his plan to set up a base there before trying to fight his way inland to the Holy City. Saladin moved his army down the coast on Richard's heels, doing him all the harm he could on the way. While his soldiers fought to delay the English King, his engineers went ahead to tear down the walls of Jaffa and to destroy the harbor so that it would be useless when Richard got there.

It was at the village of Arsouf, about fifteen miles from Jaffa, that Richard won his nickname of the Lionhearted. Saladin wanted to gain time for his engineers to finish their work of destruction, so he attacked. The battle began well for the Crusaders. They broke the Saracen cavalry with a charge, and chased them off the battlefield. They rode after them for two miles,

119

knocking the flying Saracen horsemen out of their saddles and spearing any infantrymen they came across. It was a fine gallop across level ground. It ended when the Crusaders came to the foot of the steep wooded hills which rose on the inland side of the coastal plain. Here the knights reined in their horses and watched the Saracens scrambling up the slopes among the rocks and trees. The ground all round them was covered with weapons thrown away by the enemy. Everywhere they looked they saw riderless horses bucketing about in confusion. It looked like a complete victory to them.

But when the Saracens got a short way up the hillside, they paused and looked back. They could see that the Christian knights had broken formation, as they almost always did in battle, and that they were scattered over the field in little groups around the banners of their chief barons and nobles. And they could see, too, just how few of them there were. The Saracen army had been routed by a group of Christian knights of about one tenth its size. The Saracens came swarming down the slopes again to wipe out their disgrace.

Richard saw that the battle was taking a new turn and raced into action on Fauvel, accompanied by his personal bodyguard of fifteen knights. Wherever he saw a band of knights surrounded and in trouble, he fought his way through to them, scattered their attackers and led them back to join forces with another band. In spite of all the enemy could do, Richard finally pulled the Christians together and late in the afternoon they were able to charge again as a solid mass. This time they kept their ranks and made themselves masters of the battlefield. Saladin's army vanished into the hills, and Richard went on to Jaffa unmolested.

When he got there, he was bitterly disappointed. The Saracens had done their work of destruction only too well. Long stretches of the town wall were almost flattened, and the guard towers were fire-blackened shells. Richard knew he could not move on to Jerusalem until Jaffa was refortified. He had to have a secure base. And when he had that, he would have to fight a long campaign. His fights with Saladin's army had shown him that the only safe way to get to Jerusalem would be by leapfrogging from one stronghold to another. He would have to capture the castles along the Jerusalem road, one by one.

It did not look as though he would have the

122

time or the means to do it. He did not have enough money to rebuild Jaffa and to keep his army fed and paid. The Duke of Burgundy dunned him for pay for the French. When Richard failed to get it, he threatened to take his men home. The poorer knights in the English army wanted to go home too. The Genoese and Pisan sailors who were garrisoning Acre quarreled among themselves, and fought. Richard had to hurry up there from Jaffa to make peace between them.

Richard also tried to make peace with Saladin. He met Saladin's son, El Adil, and they went hunting together with falcons on their wrists. They talked freely in the hunting field and around their campfires in the evening. Richard said that if Saladin would give up Jerusalem and all land west of the Jordan, he would

123

take his armies home and there would be no more fighting. Saladin refused these terms, but he sent El Adil a message telling him to keep on talking peace as long as he could. There was a fresh Saracen army coming from Turkestan, and he wanted to give it time to arrive before he fought Richard again.

So Richard's friendly days with El Adil went on. Richard became very fond of the young Saracen and of the manly Moslem way of living. At last he made a proposal that Saladin was willing to try. Richard suggested that El Adil should marry his sister Joanna. If Saladin would give his half of the Kingdom of Jerusalem to Joanna as a wedding present, then Richard would give the Christian half on the sea coast to El Adil. The Moslems and the Christians in the Kingdom would respect each other's Holy

Places, pilgrims of both religions would come and go as they pleased, and all would be well. It looked like a settlement. The only trouble was that Richard hadn't said anything about it to Joanna. And when she learned of the plan, she refused to marry an infidel. So the whole scheme fell through. El Adil rode back into the hills, and the friendly days came to an end.

October went by, and November. Cold winds blew off the gray sea, and it rained, day after day. The Crusaders' tents rotted, and their stores molded and spoiled. More knights went home. The Duke of Burgundy and the French muttered about Richard's dealings with El Adil and talked of treason.

Richard decided to march toward Jerusalem, more to keep the army together than with any hope of taking it. In January he had reached

125

Richard became very fond of El Adil the young Saracen.

Beit Nuba, only twelve miles from Jerusalem itself. A spy from the Holy City rode into the Christian camp with bad news. Saladin's new army from Turkestan had arrived. Richard sent for maps of Jerusalem and brooded over them

126

for a long time. It was a place that would stand a long siege. The Crusaders did not have enough men to surround it. And even if they did try to besiege it, their supply route back to Jaffa would be constantly threatened by Saladin's army which was still in the hills watching Richard, and still strong.

Richard put the maps of Jerusalem away and ordered a retreat to the coast. He made plans to spend the rest of the winter rebuilding the ruined castle at Ascalon south of Jaffa. The best he could do was to make the Christian hold on the coast as strong as possible.

At Ascalon the Christian army began to fall apart even faster than it had at Jaffa. Because money was so short, everyone, the King included, had to take a hand in rebuilding the walls that the Saracens had thrown down. The

127

Duke of Austria and his German knights refused to share the work. Richard sent for him and asked him why he was shirking. The Duke said he was neither a mason nor a carpenter. He smiled, and added that he was willing to let the baseborn do base work. He turned to go; and Richard, falling once more into one of his furies, flattened him with a kick on the backside. The Duke went home with his knights as soon after this as he could get a boat.

A little later Conrad, the French choice for King of Jerusalem, was murdered. He was going home, unarmed, after taking dinner with the fighting Bishop of Beauvais, when two men dressed as monks rode up alongside him as if they were going to speak to him and knifed him. They galloped away into the darkness and no one ever knew who they were or why they

128

killed Conrad. But almost everyone remembered that the French King had forced him on
Richard, and they believed the false monks were
Richard's men. More knights left Richard on
this account.

And now the worst news of all came to hand.
A small ship, not much bigger than a fishing
smack, arrived from England with an English
priest on board. He was a special messenger from
Richard's chief minister. He reported that Richard's younger brother John had seized his treasury, and that there was good reason to believe
that Philip Augustus was getting ready to help
John set himself up as King of England. Whatever else the news might mean, one thing was
certain. There would be no more money and
no more support for the Crusade from England
or from France.

10

The Last Wild Fight
for Jaffa

WHEN THE WINTER WAS OVER, RICHARD DECIDED on one last gamble before he went home. If Saladin had been having as much trouble as he had himself in keeping his army together through the endless months of cold and rain, the road to Jerusalem might be open. New information from spies made Richard feel that if he could get to the gates of the Holy City there would be a very good chance of getting into it. The spies said that the siege of Acre had shaken Saladin's nerve, and though he was as ready as ever to fight in the open he was determined never to let himself be shut up inside

130

a walled town. Richard felt he had a chance to bluff Saladin into giving up Jerusalem. He was sure that when the news reached England and France that the Holy Sepulchre was once again in Christian hands, plenty of men and plenty of money would be found for its defense.

Richard marched up the road from Jaffa once more and set up a camp at Beit Nuba. For several weeks he piled up siege engines, equipment, and stores, as if he were getting ready for a long siege. Saladin's patrols reported every move the Christians made, and the Moslems became convinced that Richard was going to try to take Jerusalem. Saladin's Emirs made him promise that he would not let himself be trapped in the city. They wanted him to stay outside it so that he could attack the Christians from the rear while the men from Turkestan defended the walls. The Saracens from Turkestan knew the story of Acre, too. They announced that if Saladin left Jerusalem they would march out with him.

Saladin was in despair. The Crusaders were only fifteen miles away, and he had no troops he could rely on to defend the city. He went to the Mosque of El Aksa and spent the day there in silent prayer. A watcher who saw him kneeling all day in the mosque said that his cheeks were wet with tears. In the evening he came out calm and resigned; he had given the city into the keeping of Allah. As he stepped out of the cool shadows of the mosque, a messenger greeted him in the name of Allah the Merciful and Compassionate. He came from the cavalry patrols watching the Christian camp. He said that early that morning the Crusaders had marched out of their camp in full battle

132

order. They had formed up on the crests of the hills looking down at Jerusalem, and after standing there for some hours, had faced about and marched off toward Jaffa.

Saladin spent a sleepless night waiting for more news. In the morning he heard what had happened from a spy who had slipped out of the Christian camp. Richard had learned that Saladin had blocked every sweet-water well and destroyed all the cisterns and water tanks in the farms and villages within miles of the city. That meant that, while his troops laid siege to Jerusalem, he would have to bring every drop of water for his men and his horses up twenty miles of road from beyond Beit Nuba. Richard saw that it was out of the question and started down to the coast.

The Christian army simply fell apart after this disappointment. The French under the Duke

133

of Burgundy went north to Syria; most of the English knights went home by sea from Jaffa. Richard went to Acre.

Saladin saw that he had his chance to destroy what little remained of the Christian Kingdom of Jerusalem. He swept down on Jaffa and captured the city inside three days. A few Christians held out in the citadel, but the rest of the town was lost.

Richard was packing up for the journey back to England when he heard the news. "As God lives," he said, "I will go there." He called for volunteers. The Earl of Leicester and fifty-five knights were all he could raise. They set out for Jaffa to save the people in the citadel. They had 400 men-at-arms and 2,000 bowmen with them to set against Saladin's army of nearly twenty thousand.

Head winds, followed by flat calms, held

them up as they made their way to Jaffa in galleys. When they arrived, they could see that all its churches were smouldering ruins, and that Moslem banners were flying everywhere. There was no flag flying on the citadel. Richard's ships hung back at the harbor mouth. It looked as if they were too late.

Then a man was seen sliding and scrambling down the citadel walls. He raced across the beach and plunged into the sea. One of the galleys rowed into the harbor basin and grabbed him out of the water, thinking they would save one Christian life at least. The swimmer was a priest. He said that the defenders were still holding out, but that they were at their last gasp and could only hold on for a few hours at most. Richard gave the order to land at once.

The Saracens in the town were busy looting its shops and houses, and they were taken

135

by surprise when Richard and his little band burst in on them. They ran for their lives. As they ran, they spread the rumor that Richard was back with a thousand knights. The rumors snowballed. Richard had ten thousand knights. He was killing every Saracen in the town. A panic spread. Then Richard's leopard banner unfurled and billowed out over the citadel. The rumors were true. Richard really was back. The Saracens poured out of the city gates toward Saladin's camp. The panic spread to the camp. Soon the whole army was off into the hills as fast as it could go. Saladin and his generals tried to halt their men, but they were powerless to stop them. The army melted away.

Richard made the most of his luck. None of his horses were ashore, but he managed to find three in Jaffa. He mounted one, and with two other knights rode off in pursuit of the Saracens.

The few Moslems who had rallied round Saladin and his generals bolted when they saw him coming. That night Richard pitched his tent where Saladin had been encamped the day before. Richard's tiny force had routed the whole Saracen army. Many of Saladin's commanders were so full of admiration for this feat of arms that they rode into Richard's camp under flags of truce that evening to congratulate him. Richard feasted them royally on foods taken from Saladin's abandoned kitchens, and they sang and talked in soldierly friendship until the camp-fires burned low.

It took Saladin three days to rally his army. Then he came in for a final settlement with the Christians. By this time Richard had scoured the neighborhood for everything on four legs that could be called a horse, and he had managed to mount fifteen knights. Another galley

137

with two or three hundred infantrymen had come down from Acre. But the Christians were still outnumbered by nearly ten to one.

Richard drew his army up on a piece of level ground just outside Jaffa. They were in a hedgehog formation. The outer ring was made up of spearmen kneeling behind their shields with their spears butted into the ground, points outward at an angle of forty-five degrees. Beside each spearman there was a man with a crossbow and behind him a loader. As soon as each crossbowman fired, the loader took his weapon and handed him another ready to fire. Charge after charge by the Saracen cavalry broke against the hedgehog. Toward midday Richard made his first charge with ten knights. They hit a squadron of Saracen cavalry from Turkestan and scattered them. As they turned to ride

138

back into the hedgehog, a mob of infantry rushed them. The Earl of Leicester's horse was killed under him, and down he went under a mob of Saracens. Richard went to the rescue alone, swinging his war axe. He killed a dozen Saracens and brought the Earl out of the melee. On their way back to safety inside the ring of spearmen they picked up a riderless horse which made up for the one the Earl had lost.

There was a pause in the battle soon after Richard had rescued the Earl. In the middle of it an unarmed Saracen rider leading two beautifully harnessed Arab horses trotted up to the Christians. Saladin's son El Adil had seen the wretched plug Richard was riding, and in admiration of his heroism, sent him horses more worthy of him. Richard's knights thought it was some kind of trick, and begged Richard not to use the gift horses. But the King said if the devil himself turned up with a good horse on such a day he would mount it.

A little while later bad news from inside Jaffa was brought to Richard. The Genoese sailors who had been guarding its walls had given way under Saracen attacks and were going back on board their ships. So Richard left the Earl of Leicester in command of the hedgehog and galloped off to drive the Saracens out of Jaffa again. He took two knights and two archers with him. He rallied the sailors as they milled in panic round their galleys, and then whipped the Saracens through the streets and out of the town. Then he galloped back to see how the hedgehog was getting on.

The Earl and his men were being pressed hard, and Richard saw that it was time to win them a breather. He lined up twelve knights and charged out. The Saracens stood up to the charge better this time, and soon had Richard surrounded. It looked like the end, but Richard struck a famous blow that saved the day. A Saracen knight rode out of the enemy ranks and bore down on Richard to finish him off. Richard sat himself in the saddle to meet him with his broadsword raised. As the Saracen closed with him, the great sword flashed down. The Saracens gasped. Richard had cut their champion clean through from the shoulder to the waist. His head, his shoulder, and his sword arm flew off his body. The dead man sat in the saddle for a second, and then slumped off sideways as his frightened horse bolted. The Saracens fell back from Richard in awe.

Richard rode back into his little ring of men. He knew he could not keep up the fight forever. Another really determined attack from

*Richard rode out, his lance proudly lifted
as if he were at a parade.*

the Saracens would do the trick. His tiny army
would be wiped out, and with it would go what
little was left of the Kingdom of Jerusalem. He

stared across at the enemy to see what their next move was going to be. He saw an astonishing sight. Saladin himself was riding among his troops begging them to make one more attack on the Christians. And his men were refusing. Richard suddenly knew in his bones that the enemy were licked. He rode out of his ring of spearmen alone, with his lance proudly lifted as if he were at a parade. He trotted his horse slowly from end to end of the Saracen line, but not a man would come out to meet him. Saladin's army had no more fight left in it. The old Saracen leader saw that his hopes of wiping out the Kingdom of Jerusalem had been brought to nothing. He made a peace with Richard that left Jaffa and Acre to the Christians. Richard had won a great deal in his last, wild fight at Jaffa.

11

The Fourth Great Pilgrimage

GEOFFROY DE VILLEHARDOUIN, MARSHAL OF Champagne, is often credited with having the idea of the Fourth Crusade. The fighting between Richard of England and Philip Augustus of France had come to an end. Many men-at-arms were left nothing to do when the armies of the two kings broke up, and bands of them drifted into the country of the Count of Champagne. They were ill-disciplined and troublesome. To Geoffroy it seemed a good thing for them to become part of a crusading army.

Others had the idea of a crusade about the same time. These were the French barons who had guessed wrong in choosing sides in the war between Richard and Philip Augustus and had fought with the English. They feared that the French King would punish them. Under pretense of holding a tournament they met together at Ecri to discuss what they had better do to escape punishment. They decided that Philip Augustus would not raise his hand against men who had "taken the cross." So at the end of the tournament they all "took the cross" together.

Pope Innocent III called the Crusade and sent Fulk of Neuilly to preach it, but it was a bad time to call a crusade. The war between Richard and Philip Augustus had used up much French and English treasure. There were few men left in France or England rich enough to give money to the Crusaders' war chest. And Richard's successor on the English throne, King

John, took up the war with France and fought on. Thus neither country was able to support the Crusade with men, ships or money. At the end of two years the leaders of the Crusade decided to send envoys to Venice to see if that republic would back the Crusade. Geoffroy was sent by the Count of Champagne as chief of these envoys and as spokesman.

He arrived in Venice and after much talk came to terms with the Doge and his council. They agreed to supply shipping for 4,500 horses and 30,000 men, along with food and fodder for nine months, in return for payment of 85,000 marks. They also said they would send fifty warships to escort the fleet, and a strong force of marines to serve with the army, if Geoffroy would agree to halve with them any spoils taken or land captured. Geoffroy agreed to all this.

146

Pope Innocent sent five thousand marks in silver so that the Venetians could start making their fleet ready at once. An embarkation date was set for St. John's Day in the following year, 1202. It seemed that a good beginning had been made when Geoffroy went back to Champagne to report to the Count of Champagne. But when he reached home, he found the Count ill. A short time after he died.

The Count had been the moving spirit of the Crusade, and now that he was dead things began to go wrong. He had gathered a great sum of money for the Crusade, but under his will a great part of this was now divided among his followers. Many of the Barons of Champagne who were ready enough to go overseas with him now dropped out. It was difficult to find a new leader. The Duke of Burgundy refused and

147

so did the Count of Bar-le-Duc. The fighting between King John of England and Philip Augustus was in the balance, and few great men were willing to leave France at such a troubled time. At last Boniface of Montferrat agreed to take the leadership, and at Eastertime most of the French party were ready to set out for Venice.

When the French arrived in Venice, their troubles really began. In the first place, though the Venetians had carried out their side of the bargain as far as the fleet and the supplies were concerned, the French had not carried out theirs. When they pooled their money, they found they had just half what was due the Venetians. In the second place, they found that the Venetians were making their own plans for the Crusade. The French wanted to sail to Egypt to take Cairo from the Saracens. It was their richest city, and the center of their power. If the Crusaders held it, they would find it easy to recapture the Holy Land. But the Venetians had trade treaties with the Saracens of Cairo from which they made much profit, and they did not want to lose this business. Moreover, they had made a secret treaty with Saphadin, Saladin's brother, promising that they would turn the Crusaders away from Egypt.

The Venetians dealt smoothly and shrewdly, and the French were outwitted. When the French arrived, they were given a good camp on the Island of St. Nicholas. When they were installed in it, they found the Saracens were the only ones who had the boats. This meant there was no getting off the island without their help. When the French talked of breaking up the Crusade and going home, the blind Doge of Venice, Dandolo, came to them and made a proposal. The King of Hungary, who was at war with the Venetian republic, had not long before captured the port of Zara from the Venetians. Dandolo said that the Venetians would consider that the debt would be paid if the French recaptured Zara for them. The French agreed.

In November they sailed across the Adriatic Sea to Zara. Many barons deserted before sailing, and others took to their beds and pretended to be sick. They did this so that they would not take part as Crusaders in an attack on the Christian people of Hungary. When the French reached Zara, the Abbot of Vaux came to tell them that Pope Innocent had forbidden them to attack the city; but the French had given their oath to the Doge and could not go back on it. When the Pope heard that they had taken Zara after five days of fighting, he placed them all under the ban of excommunication. It was a strange beginning to a crusade, and it disheartened more of the Crusaders. A number of them, angry with Venetian trickery, went over to join the army of the King of Hungary.

Now that the Crusaders had finished their business at Zara, they might have been expected to move on to Egypt or the Holy Land to fight the Saracens. But the many barons who had left took their money with them, and the Crusaders were poorer than before. The Doge Dandolo helped them out of their difficulties again, in his fashion. He brought Alexius Angelus to them, a man with a good claim to the throne of the Byzantine Empire who had been done out of his rights when his father, the emperor, was driven into exile by rebels. He said that if the Crusaders would restore him to his throne he would pay 200,000 marks, give a year's supplies, and lend ten thousand soldiers to take part in an attack on Cairo. The Crusaders agreed, thinking that they would get to Egypt most surely if they went first to Constantinople.

They got there toward the end of June in 1203. As the fleet sailed up close to the city, each ship hoisted the battle flags of the barons on board, and the knights hung their brightly painted shields over the sides to make a show of color and strength. But if the Greeks in the city wondered at the fleet, those on board marveled at the sight of the town. There were more people watching from the walls than the Crusaders had ever seen gathered together before. And they had never seen such fine walls or so many towers. Inside they could see more splendid palaces, churches, and great buildings than they had thought there were in all the world. Their hearts leaped at the thought of the wealth that there must be in such a splendid place. They sailed

152

along past its water front and set up camp on the far shore of the Bosporus in the old summer palace of the emperors at Chalcedon. This was another great wonder to them, because its courts and halls had room for the whole army. Never had they even heard of kings rich enough to build on such a scale. Its gardens were the most beautiful they had ever dreamed of, and they felt they had come to the noblest and fairest of cities.

After nine days spent in resting from the voyage in these lovely gardens, they began the attack on the city. The long fight lasted all through July. The Greeks fought well, and so did their mercenaries, who were mostly Englishmen and Danes armed with double-bladed battle axes. But in the end the two-handed swords of the French and the crossbows of the Venetian marines proved the better weapons. The Cru-

153

*The Crusaders sailed close to the city
of Constantinople.*

saders took Constantinople and fulfilled their promises to Alexius Angelus. He was crowned Emperor at the beginning of August.

Now it was his turn to keep his promises. But he was an unlucky man. The usurper who had been driven out had taken all the money in the treasury when he fled from the city. Shortly after Alexius' coronation a huge fire raged through Constantinople unchecked for two days and

Never had they seen such fine walls or so many towers.

nights. This, coming after the confusion and disorder of the siege, made all normal business impossible, and Alexius could not collect taxes from ruined men. When Boniface of Montferrat and the barons pressed him for the 200,000 marks he owed them, he could make only a small down payment. Months went by. When Alexius was asked for more, he had to confess that he was penniless. In January, 1204, the Crusaders

155

decided they had done all they could for him for nothing and marched out of the town, leaving him to shift for himself.

Alexius did not last long after they left. The citizens hated him for causing the siege and the disaster that had followed it. A mob invaded his palace almost as soon as the Crusaders had left the city. After keeping poor Alexius in a dungeon for a few days, the mob leader strangled him with his own hands and proclaimed himself emperor.

Now a murderer was on the Byzantine throne, which seemed against all law and justice. The Crusaders decided that such a thing should not be and drove out this upstart in April. The Greeks of the city opposed them and fought bitterly, so that when the Crusaders were victorious, they felt that the city was theirs by right of conquest. The Crusaders took what they wanted to settle the claim they had on the Emperor Alexius. It seemed that never since the beginning of the world was so much booty won in a single city. They filled three big churches with gold and silver, with jewels and precious stones, with silks, and furs, and every other precious thing. When it had all been counted, the Crusaders paid off the Venetians, and divided what was left among themselves. There was plenty for everybody. When they had divided the treasure, they divided the land of the emperors of Constantinople, and their titles. Baldwin of Flanders was crowned emperor, and Boniface of Montferrat became King of Salonika. Others took dukedoms and lordships.

Surely now the Crusaders could go to the Holy Land to free the city of Jerusalem from the Saracens! But that was not to be. They were attacked by Johannizza, King of the Bulgars

157

and Wallachs, whose lands lay at each side of the mouth of the Danube to the north of Constantinople. The Greeks hated the Crusaders so much for setting themselves over them as masters that they sided with Johannizza, even though many of his men were heathen Cumans from South Russia. So a long war began, in which towns were taken and lost and taken again as the luck went one way or the other.

After a year the luck began to run more and more against the Crusaders. They gave up most of their newly won lands to Johannizza, and at Easter in 1205 their emperor, Baldwin of Flanders, was taken prisoner in a battle outside Andrianople in which a great number of his followers were killed. Seven thousand of the Crusaders went back to France in disgust about this time, saying that they were ruining the Greeks and doing themselves no good.

Montferrat was killed in an ambush. A band of Bulgarian horsemen had surprised him without his armor on. At the beginning of the fight a Bulgar bowman planted an arrow in his upper arm, just below the shoulder. The arrow cut an artery, and within a few minutes Montferrat fainted from loss of blood and fell from his horse. When his men saw him fall, they panicked and fled.

And so after six years the Fourth Crusade came to an end in the Balkan mountains. The Venetians were well pleased. The Greek merchants who were their great rivals were ruined, and their Saracen friends in Cairo had got off scot-free. In all that time the Crusaders had never set eyes on a Saracen soldier, nor set foot on Saracen ground. For all the hard knocks they had given and taken, they got little but honor as fighting men.

159

12

The Crusades of Saint Louis

THE LAST CRUSADES WERE LED BY SAINT LOUIS, known also as King Louis IX of France. He took an army to Egypt almost exactly a hundred and fifty years after the Kingdom of Jerusalem was set up.

Saint Louis was in many ways a great king who did fine things for France, but he had a strange hatred of his high office. He often dreamed of giving up his crown and retiring into a monastery. But he knew that he could not give up his responsibilities. He compromised by living like a monk so far as he could. He always wore dark clothes made of the cheapest

160

Louis IX of France lived as much like a monk as possible.

materials. He ate plainly and fasted often. He would lie for hours on the cold stone floor of his private room praying, and when he was carry-

161

ing out his duties as a king he wore a rough hair shirt under his clothes.

As he grew older, he was troubled by an illness. For days at a time he would be unable to eat or sleep, and he would be tortured by muscle cramps. When these spells ended, he would fall into a coma, and lie speechless and unable to move for hours at a time. In 1244 he had an unusually bad attack; and while he lay in his trance, he heard the people watching him give up hope for his recovery. As soon as he regained his speech, he murmured a vow to go on a crusade.

His wife, his Father Confessor, the bishops of the kingdom and his chief ministers all begged him to retract the vow when he was fully recovered, but they could not move him. He was determined to go.

Times had changed. Though the King and a

company of Franciscan monks toured France preaching the Crusade, there was no enthusiasm for it. It was three years before Saint Louis could raise an army, and four years before it was ready to set out.

Louis' preparations were unusually complete. He had built a special embarkation port for the Crusade at Aigues Mortes in the south of France, and he had laid in two years' supplies of food at an advance base in Cyprus. But between Cyprus and Egypt storms scattered his fleet, and he landed at Damietta in the delta of the Nile short of men and short of supplies. He hesitated for a time by the seacoast and then tried to fight his way through to Cairo. The Sultan was dying, and Saint Louis hoped he would be able to capture the town while the Saracens were divided by disputes about who should succeed him.

163

But in a century and a half the knights had learned nothing new about war, and the Saracens had learned a great deal. The knights still relied on their charges to break up any battle line that tried to stand up against them. They had improved their helmets a little, and the more advanced knights wore plate armor on their shoulders and on their knees for extra protection. But nothing else had been done to improve their fighting capabilities. The Saracens had been learning all the time. They had found out how to fight in disciplined companies with a chain of command coming down from a single leader in the field. Their generals had learned how to get orders to their men on the battlefield so that they could change their plans as the fortunes of war ebbed and flowed.

Saint Louis and his army soon found themselves cut off from their base at Damietta and surrounded at Mansûra. When they tried to break out of the Saracen ring, they were outfought and driven back. The Nile ran slowly past their camp in the marshy, unhealthy delta. Thousands of flies crawled all over their food. Disease broke out. The French King was so weak that he had to be lifted onto his horse. He could hardly hold up his head under his heavy silver helmet ornamented with golden lilies. Tottering in his saddle, he led one more effort to break out toward Damietta and the sea. Halfway through the battle he fainted and was carried into a house to lie down. His knights fought bravely, but they were outmatched. As soon as the Saracens tired, bugles sounded and drums rolled. Their weary squadrons trotted away, and fresh men on fresh horses galloped up to carry on the fight. The

165

knights were worn down and exhausted, and their sickness took the heart out of them. After a few hours they gave in and surrendered.

The King of France lay that night in chains on a bed of straw in a prison called the House of Lockmar. His whole army slept near by, penned up in sheds and courtyards. In the following days, the Saracens massacred all his men-at-arms who would not become Moslems, and marched those who would off to the slave markets in Cairo. Saint Louis and his knights were allowed to buy their freedom. But the ransom was a huge sum of money and many knights were ruined raising their share of it. They sailed home in rags. All their fine arms and armor were lost, their horses, and their embroidered tents. Their squires and men-at-arms were all dead or enslaved, and many of their friends were left behind, dead in battle or of the plague. It was a complete defeat.

Saint Louis could not bear to go home with so little done. He sailed up the coast of Palestine to the Kingdom of Jerusalem and spent several years there, strengthening its castles, and building new strongholds on its boundaries.

But it was all of little use. The Saracens had a new leader, greater even than Saladin, the Sultan Beibars. He was a huge man, red-haired like Richard the Lionhearted, with one bright blue eye in his head. He had lost the other in battle. He was a Tartar from inner Asia who had once been sold in the slave market at Damascus for about a hundred dollars. His first buyer returned him to the dealer when he found he was walleyed, and someone else snapped him up as a bargain. He turned out to be a good one, for he was a dead shot with a crossbow and a master of all weapons. He worked his way up in the service of the Saracens in Egypt until he became commander of the Sultan's bodyguard. In the end he became Sultan. When Saint Louis at last had to go home to see to his affairs in France, Beibars took Jaffa and Antioch. All that was left of the three Christian Kingdoms in the Holy Land was a little stretch of country round Acre.

Saint Louis led one more Crusade. Toward the end of the year 1269 the Moslem Emir in charge of the fortress town of Tunis in North Africa sent messages to Saint Louis saying that his country was stricken by famine. He would surrender the town, and he would become a Christian if the French would come bringing food with them. As proof of his good faith, he sent a large payment of gold with his message.

Saint Louis thought he might exchange Tunis for Antioch if he could get possession of it, and he tried to raise an army. But France had not forgotten the bitter defeat at Mansûra. Very few knights were willing to go. At last Saint Louis set out with only a thousand knights and a fleet of only fifty-five ships.

When he reached Tunis, he found that he had been lured into a trap. The Moslem Emir had no intention of giving up the city, and he had thousands of good troops waiting and ready to fight. The Crusaders went into camp close to the ruins of ancient Carthage, among the salt marshes. The summer heat was intense, dust storms swept through camp incessantly, and once again thousands of flies crawled over the Crusaders' food and rubbish. Within a week the plague had broken out. The Papal legate with the expedition died. Saint Louis' own son, Jean

Saint Louis' last words were, "Oh Jerusalem, Jerusalem."

Tristram, died, and hundreds of others died with them. In the end Louis himself fell sick. "God have mercy on these Thy people, lead them into safety in their own land," he prayed on his sick-bed. He lay in silence for a long time, and then murmured, "Oh Jerusalem, Jerusalem." They were his last words.

The Crusaders broke camp and went home. A day out of Tunis a storm came up and scattered the little fleet. A third of the ships were wrecked on the Sicilian coast and hundreds of men were drowned in the surf. There was plague aboard the ships that survived; and as they sailed on toward France, more and more Crusaders fell sick and died. When they reached friendly harbors at last, they counted their losses. Saint Louis' brother and his wife were dead; his daughter Isabelle and her husband, the King of Navarre, were dead; many more barons and knights were dead or dying. The news spread through France. Tunis, after Mansûra, gave the Crusades an evil name. No more armies set out for the Holy Land.

The midget Kingdom of Jerusalem lingered on for another twenty years before the Saracens took Acre and swept it way. Eight years after that a Mongol horde from inner Asia swept across the Saracen countries and came into Syria. Their Great Khan sent the Pope a letter from his camp at Damascus, saying that if a Christian army came to help him fight the Saracens of Egypt he would pay them by restoring the Kingdom of Jerusalem. Two years went by and his letter in its strange Chinese-looking writing remained unanswered. He wrote again and made the same offer. Again there was no answer, and no Christians came to win back the Holy Sepulchre. The Great Khan and his horde rode back to their plains in Asia, and the chance was lost. The Crusades were over.

13

After the Crusades

ALL THROUGH THE HOLY LAND THE GREAT CASTLES
of the Crusaders stand, slowly crumbling away
in the long hot summers and the short hard
winters. But the Crusaders left few other traces
behind them. The knights who lived in the
castles made little mark on the life of the country.
It was the other way round. When they had been
there a little time, they fell in love with the
Moslem way of living; with the Saracen houses,
with their shady courtyards and their fountains,
with the loose, comfortable, flowing robes of the
Easterners. They forgot their Western ways and
began to melt into the East. After one or two
173

generations they seemed very foreign to the Crusaders fresh from Europe, and the Crusaders
seemed rough and barbaric to them.

The earlier Crusaders were astonished by the
habits of the important men they met in the
East. The Europeans rarely took baths, and they
were surprised to find that the Easterners had
kept the old Roman habit of going to public baths
to exercise and take hot and cold plunges afterward. They found that the Moslems, too, had
the same fetish for cleanliness. The Saracens, in
fact, were under a religious obligation to clean
themselves every day, and very thoroughly too.
It all seemed very effeminate and unmanly to
the Europeans. So did the business of reading
and writing. To the Crusaders from the North
that was a priest's trick, and unmanly. A knight
had no time to learn such things, and no need
for such knowledge. He could always hire some

174

clerk in orders to keep his records for him. The Crusaders were surprised to find that the nobles at the Byzantine court not only knew how to read, but wrote too, and often wrote poems and songs as well. They could go to the universities and argue and chop logic with scholars. Frequently they did so for their amusement. The Crusaders pretended to despise the Byzantine nobles for their learning, but secretly it impressed them. When they went home, they took back the idea that a noble should be a cultivated man as well as a good fighter. They began to give their children tutors as well as masters-at-arms. The Crusaders did a good deal to civilize the knights.

But on the whole the Crusades did very little to change European ways. The precious works of art that the Crusaders took home did not do much to change styles in Europe. While the

Crusades were going on, Gothic art flowered. It was too different from Byzantine art to take much from it in the way of influences. What came back from the East with the Crusaders was more of an idea of luxury that they had taken from the Greeks of Antioch and Constantinople. They saw how comfortably the Byzantines lived, and they wanted houses that were as well built and as convenient. The castles of the nobles at the beginning of the Crusades were little more than permanent camps. As the Crusades went on, more and more people began to have an idea of living comfortably. But their new ideas were translated into Gothic terms—they didn't imitate the Byzantine way of building; they found their own way.

Perhaps the most important thing they learned about was government. The Byzantines had kept the old Roman civil service almost without

176

change. The Emperor at Constantinople had ministries and bureaus that kept a tight control over national life. The Crusaders lived under the feudal system, each lord governed his own neighborhood and was responsible to the duke or count to whom he had sworn allegiance. The dukes or counts ruled their domains as they would, and their kings had very little authority over them. The kings who went to the East saw that the emperor ruled without being challenged by feudal nobles; he was an absolute ruler and he had authority over the whole state. The European kings brought back with them the idea of making themselves as powerful in their domains.

They saw, too, that the emperor in Constantinople was much more important than any priest in his dominions. The Byzantine church had no authority like the Pope, for the emperor himself

177

was head of the church. The kings took that idea back with them too. They were no longer willing to allow the priests and bishops in their kingdoms to claim freedom from their laws and commands.

And they were no longer willing to accept the Pope's authority as greater than theirs. Before the Crusades the people of western Europe lived as members of Christendom—they were Christians first, and owed allegiance to the Pope. After that came their allegiance to their feudal lord. The king was far away, and the idea of nation and country was dim and vague. All that changed while the Crusades were going on. The idea of the state and the nation grew stronger, and the idea of Christendom grew weaker. On the First Crusade everyone wore the same red cross. On the Third Crusade the French had red crosses, the English white ones, and the men from Flanders and Lorraine green crosses. Men were beginning to think they owed more to their kings and their countries than they did to the Church.

The most lasting effects of the Crusades were commercial and political. The Fourth Crusade, that so strangely turned into an attack on Constantinople, ruined the splendid city. The Byzantines never recovered from it. Their trade passed into the hands of the Venetians, and their city began to wither and die. Great cities and empires die slowly, and Constantinople lingered on, half alive, inside its massive Roman walls for two hundred and fifty years. Then the Moslems battered down its walls with heavy cannon, and the Byzantine Empire died at last. The consequences were that Greece and all the Balkan countries, once the richest Roman provinces, became Moslem colonies. Most of their Christian inhabitants were ruled by Moslems until less than a hundred years ago. Constantinople is still a Turkish city. That the flag of Islam floats over the city founded by the first Christian Emperor of Rome is largely due to Villehardouin and the men of the Fourth Crusade.

180

Index

Acre: Accursed Tower, 106, 109-10, 112, 114-15; capture of, 106-15, 143; *map*, 35
Adalais, sister of Philip Augustus of France, 99
Adhemar de Monteil, 15-18, 31, 44
Adil, El, 123-25, 139
Adrianople, 158
Adriatic Sea, 44, 150
Africa, Moslem conquest of, 5-6
Aigues Mortes, France, 163
Aleppo, 38, 61, 81
Alexius Angelus, 151, 154-57
Alexius Commenus, 31, 39-42, 44-45, 47, 52
Allah, 132
Almohades, dominions of, *map*, 34
Angevins, dominions of, *map*, 34
Antioch: Beibars' capture, 168; Bohemond of Taranto, prince, 66; buildings, 58; captures, 60-61, 168; cedars, 59; mineral resources, 59; riches, 58-59; soil, 59; streets, 58; tolerance, 59; trade, 58-59; Turkish siege, 61-64; walls, 58
Apulia, *map*, 34-35
Arabs: civilizing of, 7; conquests, 5-6, 9; Turkish conquest of, 10-11
Aragon, *map*, 34

Armenia, *map*, 35
Armenian Christians, 56
Ascalon, 127; *map*, 35
Asia, 11, 32
Asia Minor, 7
Austria, Duke of, 128
Austria, *map*, 34

Balkan(s), 76
Balkan Mountains, 21
Baltic Sea, 6
Bar-le-Duc, Count of, 148
Barbarians: civilizing of, 7; Europe, conquest of, 4
Beauvais, Bishop of, 128
Beibars, Sultan, 167-68
Beit Nuba, 126, 131, 133
Belgrade, 21, 23-24, 27; *map*, 35
Berengaria, wife of Richard I, 99
Bernard of Clairvaux, Saint, 74-76, 79, 86
Bible, 15
Biscay, Bay of, 95
Black Sea, 8; *map*, 35
Bohemond of Taranto, 64-66, 72
Boniface of Flanders, 157
Boniface of Montferrat, 148, 155, 157, 159
Bosporus, 32, 153

181

Bouillon, Godfrey de, 18, 45, 47, 66, 71
Boulogne, Baldwin of, 15-16, 56-57
Bowmen, 108
Breteuil, Walter of, 20, 28
Bulgaria, *map*, 35
Burel, Geoffrey, 20, 26, 28, 33, 39, 41
Burgundy, 75, 95
Burgundy, Duke of, 116-17, 123, 125, 133-34, 147
Byzantine Christians, Turkish persecution of, 32
Byzantine Empire: Church, authority of, 177-78; emperors, *see* Alexius Angelus, Alexius Commenus, Boniface of Flanders, Manuel; government, 176-77; *map*, 35; throne, claim to, 151; Turkish menace, 12
Byzantium. *See* Constantinople

Caeserea, *map*, 35
Cairo, 163, 166; *map*, 35
Catapults, 109
Castile, *map*, 34
Chalcedon, 47, 153
Champagne, Count of, 144
Channel Coast, 16
Christ, 9
Cistercian Monks, 74, 79-80
Civetot, 33, 38, 42-43, 48
Clement, Aubrey, 114
Clermont, France, 13-14
Cluny monastery, 12
Constantinople, 7, 11, 22-23, 32, 35, 44-45, 152-53, 180
Converts, fanaticism of, 11
Corsica, *map*, 34
Crete, 100; *map*, 34
Crusade(s): European ways, changing, 175-80; last, 160-72; reasons for, 3-8; results, 173-80; *See also*

First Crusade; Second; Third; Fourth
Crusaders: armaments, 49-50, 153; crowned kings, 57, 66, 71-72; defined, 18; Eastern ways, adoption of, 173-75; mutual distrust, 64-65; oath, 18; prisoners, treatment of, 52, 118; sacking and burning, 24, 26-28, 31, 36, 38, 43, 47, 76-77
Cumans, 158; *map*, 35
Cyprus, 101-05, 163

Damascus, 61, 82-84, 167, 172; *map*, 35
Damascus, Emir of, 83-84
Damietta, Egypt, 163, 165
Dandolo, Doge of Venice, 146, 149-51
Danube River and Valley, 21, 23, 26, 158
Denmark, 6
Dracon, 40
Dracon River, 38

Ecri, France, 145
Edessa: Kingdom of, 56-73; Baldwin of Boulogne, king, 57; *map*, 35; Turks' capture, 73, 86
Egypt, Moslem conquest of, 5
El Aska Mosque, Jerusalem, 132
Engineers, 108, 113, 119
England, 95; *map*, 34
Erzgebirge, 21
Eugenius, Pope, 74, 76, 86
Euphrates Valley, 56
Europe, *map*, 34-35

Fauvel (horse), 103-05, 121
Fire pots, 109, 114
First Crusade, 11-72, 78; date, 4;

popularity, 14, 19; proclamation, 13-14; rewards for, 14-15; route, *map*, 34-35. *See also* Peter the Hermit
Flanders, 75
Flanders, Count of, 111
Fourth Crusade, 144-59; makeup, 144-45; results, 159
France, *map*, 34
Franks, 18
French barons, 75, 144-45
Fulk of Neuilly, 145

Genoa, Italy, 95
German barons, 75
Goths, 17
Great Khan, 172
Greece, 58
Greed, 36, 39

Harz Mountains, 21
Hauberks, 114
Henry II, King of England, 97
Hohenstaufen, Conrad, 75-79, 82-83, 85
Holy City. *See* Jerusalem
Holy Land, overland trail, 21-22
Holy Places, 124-25
Holy Sepulchre, Jerusalem, 9, 12, 66, 89, 131
Holy Wars. *See* Crusade(s)
Hungary, 76; *map*, 35
Hungary, King of, 150-51

Infantry, 43
Innocent III, Pope, 145, 147, 150
Ireland, *map*, 34
Isaac, King of Cyprus, 101-05
Islam (religion): appeal, 5, 7; defined, 5; (as a) faith, 5; spread

of, 5-8; unifying force, 5. *See also* Moslems

Jaffa, 68, 119, 122, 127, 135-36, 138, 143, 160
Jerusalem: Arab capture, 9; Crusaders' murder of inhabitants, 69-71; Crusaders' siege, 69-70; fortifications, 69; Godfrey de Bouillon, king, 71; *map*, 35; reputation, 15; Saladin's recapture, 92; Turkish conquest, 11
Joanna, sister of Richard I, 97, 124-25
Johannizza, King of the Bulgars and Wallachs, 157-58
John, brother of Richard I, 129, 146, 148
Jordan River and Valley, 69, 89, 123

"Kiokio," 19
"King of the bums," 43
Kurds, 11

Langres, Bishop of, 79-80
Last Crusade, 160-72
Lebanon, 68
Leicester, Earl of, 134, 139-40
Leon, *map*, 34
Limmasol, Cyprus, 101
Lockmar, House of, 166
Lorraine, 75
Louis VII, King of France, 74, 80-82, 85
Louis IX, King of France, Saint: asceticism, 160-62; crusade, 160-71
Lusignan, Guy of, 87-92, 105, 116-17
Lyons, 95

Main River, 21
Mainz, 21; *map*, 34
Mangonels, 109
Manuel, Emperor of Byzantium, 77-79, 82, 85
Mansûra, 165, 169, 171; *map*, 35
Manzikert, Battle of, 8
Marmora, Sea of, 32, 77
Marseilles, 95
Mediterranean Sea, 3, 5, 8
Messina, Sicily, 96, 99-100
Miritza Valley, 22, 30
Miners, 112
Mohammed, 5
Montferrat, Conrad of, 117, 128
Moors, *map*, 34
Morava River, 21
Moslems: Christ, respect for, 10; defined, 5. *See also* Arabs; Islam
Mosul, 61, 64
Mosul, Emir of, 73, 83

Navarre, King of, 171
Navarre, *map*, 34
Nicea, 8, 33, 35, 38-40, 48-51, 53, 55
Nile River, 165
Nish, 21-22, 27-30; *map*, 35
Normans, 16
Norway, 6
Nur-ed-din (leader), 86
Nürnberg, 21; *map*, 34

Orontes River, 59, 64

Palestine, 66
Persia, 58
Peter the Hermit, 9-44; appearance, 18-19; army, discipline, 24-26, 28-29, 31-33, 38-39; asceticism, 19; clothing, 18; Constantinople, arrival in, 31; cru-

sade, end of, 44; difficulties, blindness to, 22-23; Holy Land pilgrimage, 9-11; hopes, ruin of, 20; papal commission, 12-13; war chest, loss of, 30
Philip Augustus, King of France, 93-94, 98, 111, 116-17, 129
Philippopolis, 22; *map*, 35
Plundering, 24, 31, 36
Poland, *map*, 35
Pope, The, 12-13, 15, 172, 177-78. *See also* Eugenius; Innocent
Portugal, wars with Turks, 95; *map*, 34
Prisoners, treatment of, 52, 118
Provence, 13
Prussia, *map*, 35
Pyrenees, 14

Rainald, 33, 36, 38
Regensburg, 31; *map*, 34
Rhine Valley, 21, 95
Rhineland, 75
Rhone Valley, 95
Richard I, King of England: bravery, 121-22, 139-41; description, 93; fury, 113, 117-18, 128; horse, 101-05; luck, 136; Saladin, defeat of, 143
Robert of Normandy, 17, 66
Roi truand, 43
Roman Empire: breakup, 18; Christianization, 3-4; government, 176
Rome, 11, 58; *map*, 34
Rome, Sultan of, 8, 33, 36, 56
Roussa, sacking of, 47
Russia, *map*, 35
Russia, South, 158

Saint Nicholas Island, 149
Saladin, 87-92, 106, 115-16; defeat

by Richard I, 143; dominions, *map*, 35; Jerusalem, conquest, 92
Salonika, 157
Sans Avoir, Walter, 20, 22-23, 39-41
Saphadin, 149
Saracens. *See* Turks
Sardinia, *map*, 34
Second Crusade, 74-86; failure, 86; makeup, 75
Seljuks, *map*, 35
Semlin, 23-27; *map*, 35
Serbia, *map*, 35
Sicily, *map*, 34
Sidon, 68
Siege work, 108
Spain, wars with Moslems, 6, 12-14
Stone-throwing machines, 108
Suger, Abbot, 86
Sultan of Rome, 8, 33, 36, 56
Surcoats, 114
Sweden, Christian conversion, 6
Syria, 5, 134

Tancred, King of Sicily, 97-99
Taurus Mountains, 55
Third Crusade, 93-114; makeup, 93; results, 144
Thrace, 22, 30
Toulouse, Raymond of, 13, 17, 47, 64-66, 71
Toulouse, *map*, 34

Tristram, Jean, 169-70
True Cross, 89, 92, 116
Tunis, 168-69, 171; *map*, 34
Turk(s): Arabs, conquest of, 10-11; armaments, 49-50, 55; Byzantine Christians, persecution of, 32; Byzantine Empire, menace to, 12; cavalry, 78, 80; fanaticism, 11; Moslem conversion, 7; Seljuk, 83; tactics, improvement, 164-65
Turkestan troops, 124, 126, 131-32, 138
Typhoid fever, 65, 71
Tyre, 68; *map*, 35

Vaux, Abbot of, 150
Venice, 146, 148; *map*, 34
Vezelay (city), 95
Villehardouin, Geoffroy de, 144, 146, 180

Warrior priests, 15-16
William the Good, King of Sicily, 97

Xerigordon, siege of, 36-39

Zara, Hungary, 150-51
Zengi (leader), 86

Have you read these World Landmarks?

★

CHECK THE LIST BELOW

W-1 **The First Men in the World,** by Anne Terry White

W-2 **Alexander the Great,** by John Gunther

W-3 **The Adventures and Discoveries of Marco Polo,** by Richard J. Walsh

W-4 **Joan of Arc,** by Nancy Wilson Ross

W-5 **King Arthur and His Knights,** by Mabel L. Robinson

W-6 **Mary, Queen of Scots,** by Emily Hahn

W-7 **Napoleon and the Battle of Waterloo,** by Frances Winwar

W-8 **Royal Canadian Mounted Police,** by Richard L. Neuberger

W-9 **The Man Who Changed China,** by Pearl S. Buck

W-10 **The Battle of Britain,** by Quentin Reynolds

W-11 **The Crusades,** by Anthony West

W-12 **Genghis Khan,** by Harold Lamb

W-13 **Queen Elizabeth and the Spanish Armada,** by Frances Winwar

W-14 **Simon Bolivar,** by Arnold Whitridge

W-15 **The Slave Who Freed Haiti,** by Katharine Scherman

W-16 **The Story of Scotland Yard,** by Laurence Thompson

W-17 **The Life of Saint Patrick,** by Quentin Reynolds

W-18 **The Exploits of Xenophon,** by Geoffrey Household

W-19 **Captain Cook Explores the South Seas,** by Armstrong Sperry

W-20 **Marie Antoinette,** by Bernadine Kielty

W-21 **Shakespeare and the Globe Theater,** by Van H. Cartmell

W-22 **The French Foreign Legion,** by Wyatt Blassingame